BATMAN™
&
ROBIN™

WARNER BROS. PRESENTS

A JOEL SCHUMACHER FILM ARNOLD SCHWARZENEGGER GEORGE CLOONEY CHRIS O'DONNELL UMA THURMAN ALICIA SILVERSTONE "BATMAN & ROBIN" MICHAEL GOUGH PAT HINGLE ELLE MACPHERSON

MUSIC BY ELLIOT GOLDENTHAL EXECUTIVE PRODUCERS BENJAMIN MELNIKER AND MICHAEL E. USLAN BASED UPON DC COMICS CHARACTERS CREATED BY BOB KANE AND PRODUCED BY DC COMICS WRITTEN BY AKIVA GOLDSMAN PRODUCED BY PETER MACGREGOR-SCOTT

DIRECTED BY JOEL SCHUMACHER

WWW.BATMAN-ROBIN.COM

BATMAN™
&
ROBIN™

Novelization by ALAN GRANT

**Based on the screenplay by
AKIVA GOLDSMAN**

Batman created by Bob Kane

Little, Brown and Company
Boston   New York   Toronto   London

**To my daughter, Shalla, who's spent twenty years
explaining why she's named
after the Silver Surfer's girlfriend**

First Edition

Library of Congress Cataloging-in-Publication Data
Grant, Alan.
    Batman & Robin / novelization by Alan Grant. — 1st ed.
      p   cm.
    "Based on the screenplay written by Akiva Goldsman. Batman
created by Bob Kane."
    Summary: A new crimefighter, Batgirl, helps Batman and Robin try to
stop villains Mr. Freeze and Poison Ivy, whose nefarious plans threaten to
shred the fabric of life in Gotham City.
    ISBN 0-316-17692-3
    [1. Heroes — Fiction.   2. Adventures and adventurers — Fiction.]
I. Title
PZ7.G7666435Bat   1997
[Fic] — dc21   97-10065

10 9 8 7 6 5 4 3 2 1

COM-MO

Published simultaneously in Canada
by Little, Brown & Company (Canada) Limited

Printed in the United States of America

BATMAN™
&
ROBIN™

CHAPTER

1

In a chamber all gleaming chrome and inky shadow, a black gauntlet snapped into place. The folds of a dark cape whipped around shoulders clad in black. A bat-shaped buckle locked securely.

Deep in the Batcave, Batman was preparing for action.

Close by, a hand chose a silver Throwing Bird from a weapons array. A black eye-mask was raised into place. Tunic armor clicked shut, revealing the insignia of Robin.

Batman emerged from his costume vault into the massive grandeur of the Batcave. After the cave had been destroyed by the Riddler, a fortune had been spent on redesigning and rebuilding it. Deep excavation had virtually doubled its size. New state-of-the-art computer systems flashed, and surveillance screens monitoring news and police frequencies kept an ever-alert eye on everything that happened in Gotham City.

Through a hiss of escaping steam, Batman strode toward the pedestal that rose from the center of the cave floor. On it stood a new, sleeker, more powerful Batmobile.

Robin appeared in the doorway of his own vault, ready to follow.

A discreet cough announced the presence of Alfred Pennyworth, the butler who was entrusted with the crimefighters' secret identities. He stepped forward out of the shadows.

"Do call if you're going to be late for dinner, sir," he said in his rich English voice, as his boss slid into the Batmobile.

The Batmobile's turbos roared into life, and the vehicle shot forward through the arches of the cave access tunnel. Behind, the segmented top of the Batmobile service pedestal split wide, like the opening petals of a flower. Revealed at its center was the Redbird, Robin's newly customized motorcycle.

"Drive carefully," Alfred admonished.

Robin grinned as he settled onto the bike's saddle and gunned its engines into raucous life.

"Don't wait up, Al," he said, the words almost lost in the roar as the Redbird exploded into motion, speeding off after the Batmobile.

Alfred stood for a moment and watched them go. Then

he relaxed, leaning his weight against the main computer console. For a moment he let a great feeling of weakness wash over him, before mentally pulling himself together again. He was not as well as he seemed.

The Redbird and the Batmobile streaked down the tunnel together. "Ten police cruisers frozen solid on the Gotham Expressway," Batman reported grimly, his words instantly relayed to Robin by the sophisticated radio mikes that kept them in constant communication.

"A giant drilling truck burrowing under the city," Robin returned, scanning his own monitor.

The conclusion was inescapable — Mr. Freeze.

Robin consulted the data scrolling on his console screen. "The Batcomputer tracks him heading for the Gotham Museum."

Batman nodded. "There's a new antiquities exhibit. 'The Second Sun of the Sudan.'"

Robin recalled the news feature he'd read that morning. "Of course! Freeze is going to steal the giant white diamond!"

"No, Robin," Batman contradicted his young partner. "He's going to jail."

Seconds later, they burst out of the hidden tunnel into the night.

The Gotham Museum had been constructed in the late 1800s, during one of Gotham City's periodic booms. A stone and glass palace that had cost a king's ransom to build, it stood on the edge of Robertson Park. On this troubled night, a giant drilling truck pointed up through the rubble of the shattered floor of the museum's Great Hall, where it had come to rest. Dim light glimmered as it reflected off the drill's huge glass head.

All around was a scene from a nightmare. A model of a mighty brontosaurus, a hundred feet from head to tail, gleamed in the muted light. Frozen. Like every other exhibit in the hall. On the steps of an Aztec temple exhibit, three uniformed guards stood like statues.

The shatterproof glass of a giant diamond case suddenly started to glow blue, then white. It held for a moment, then exploded into a thousand flying fragments. High on a pyramid altar stood a silver-suited figure, his bald white head visible beneath the helmet he wore. He held a high-tech bazooka in one hand.

"The Iceman cometh," the villain known as Mr. Freeze announced archly, his voice as cold as the frigid air.

A gang of thugs in thermal suits skated to the base of the steps — the Icemen, Freeze's dangerous hirelings. Two of them held a moaning, shivering guard captive. "Please," the man begged, "show some mercy."

The very air seeming to shimmer with cold around him, Mr. Freeze started down the altar steps. "I'm afraid my condition has left me cold to your pleas," he said thinly. He fired his bazooka without warning. A beam of cryonic energy leaped from it, engulfing the guard. The heat instantly drained from the man's body, flash-freezing him and turning him into a statue of glittering ice.

Freeze tapped on the guard's frozen cheek. "Copsicle," he said, with no trace of a smile. He walked past the guard and headed for the shattered display case. "In this universe," he went on, speaking as if to himself, "there is only one absolute." He swiped away the broken glass and twisted steel, and stooped to retrieve a tremendous diamond from the debris. In one powerful hand, he raised the Second Sun of the Sudan high over his head, the gem sparkling like a star as light hit it. "Everything freezes."

Suddenly, the skylight in the high roof exploded. Batman crashed through it, free-falling down into the vast chamber. Cape streaming behind him, the Dark Knight landed on the frozen brontosaurus's neck and began to slide feet-first down its icy surface. Mr. Freeze could only stare in astonishment, as Batman came shooting off the huge beast's tail to smash into the villain's chest.

The diamond flew from Freeze's grasp and skidded across the frozen floor. Freeze coolly aimed his gun. "Bat on ice, anyone?"

But before Freeze could pull the trigger, Batman's foot lashed out. He kicked the weapon from Freeze's grasp, sending it spinning into the air. "Didn't your mother tell you never to play with guns?"

In answer, Freeze cartwheeled across the room. Coming to a sudden halt, the villain reached into the air to grab the falling weapon. "You're not sending me to the cooler!" he snarled, his finger tightening on the trigger. A solid jet of frigid energy lanced toward Batman. Even as the Dark Knight dodged the blast, Freeze took aim again.

There was a loud crash and Freeze turned to see Robin on his Redbird blast in through the museum's front doors. Robin jerked back on the handlebars, gunning the turbos, and the Redbird soared into the air. As he passed over Freeze's head, Robin lashed out with his foot at the gun. It clattered to the altar atop the giant pyramid.

"He scores!" Robin laughed. "And the crowd goes wild."

He locked the bike into a sideways skid as it came down to land. It zoomed past an exhibit, sending a priceless vase toppling. Robin reached out to grab a statue, holding tight as he whipped around it in an athletic dismount.

An instant before the vase hit the floor, Batman's

gauntleted hand reached out to snatch it to safety. Robin joined him as he replaced it on its pedestal, and together they turned to race for Freeze.

"Grab the gem," the villain commanded his henchmen. "Kill the heroes!"

Icemen in hockey masks, sticks in hand, rushed the crimefighters from both sides. Batman and Robin immediately launched into a martial arts extravaganza, ducking and weaving as the wildly swung hockey sticks arced and swooped at them. The crimefighters' fists and feet shot out time and again, to punch a jaw or clip an ankle.

Ignoring the fight, Freeze raced toward the altar and his fallen gun. Once he had it again, no one could stand up to him!

The diamond lay on the ice beyond Freeze's thugs. Simultaneously, Batman and Robin snatched the hockey sticks away from their attackers, then used them to hook the villains' ankles and upend them. The two fought as a team, each seeming to read the other's mind and know what he was going to do next.

Whatever Freeze is paying these thugs, Robin thought, *it isn't enough!*

Both heroes pressed a concealed button on their belts. Sections of their boot soles rolled back, and miniature skate blades popped out. Now they'd be on equal footing with the enemy.

Freeze had made it to his gun and he turned to fire, the energy beam creating a hoary ice bridge that stretched all the way down to the museum floor. "Caution," he quipped. "Bridge may ice over."

In perfect control, the villain slid down the bridge to the floor below and ran for his drilling truck.

"You get the ice," Batman called, decking his last opponent and turning to skate away. "I'll get the Iceman."

Batman was closing fast on Freeze when the villain turned and fired. Batman ducked, holding up his cape as a shield, deflecting the beam into an Iceman, freezing the thug solid.

Robin sped up to join Batman. "I got mine," the younger man said, holding up the diamond. "Where's yours?"

Freeze had disappeared behind the giant brontosaurus. "What killed the dinosaurs?" he asked himself, hands reaching to push against the creature's belly. "The Ice Age," he replied, muscles straining as he pushed with all his might.

The great beast toppled forward. It crashed hard to the floor in front of the oncoming Batman and Robin, the brittle body bursting like a bomb into a million icy shards.

"He's definitely extinct," Robin joked as the duo weaved and ducked to avoid the icy debris. Suddenly, an Iceman came skating in from the side. His blow missed Robin but clipped the boy's hand, sending the diamond flying free.

Freeze paused as he climbed toward the hatch of his specially modified drilling truck, drinking in the scene. The Icemen were a rushing wall between the heroes and the gem. Batman and Robin skated straight at their foes, reaching out to pull flagpoles from a display, maneuvering them as if they were about to joust with the villains.

But at the last second, they drove their poles into the ice and vaulted up over the heads of the startled Icemen. Batman and Robin came down on the landing, only feet from the Sudanese gem that Freeze wanted so badly. Even as Batman reached out for it, an Iceman's stick scythed down in a slapshot, sending the diamond whirling through the air —

To land cleanly in Mr. Freeze's glove.

"Thanks for playing." Freeze dropped down into the cab of his giant drilling machine and hit the button to close the hatch.

Batman leaped up onto the banister. "Round up the thugs," he ordered Robin. "I'll get Freeze." He vaulted up onto the truck, and threw himself through the hatch just before it slid closed.

Inside, Freeze stood at the main control console in the drill's toughened glass head. "Nice of you to drop in," he said to Batman, without even turning, as the hero landed behind him. The villain hit another button, and there was a sudden mighty roar.

The control capsule was set on the end of an ejection cylinder, and now it blasted out of the drilling truck, rising like a rocket toward the museum roof.

Robin paused at the sound. Turning from his chase, he leaped onto a handrail, slid down, grabbed a banner, and swung. Letting go at the last moment, he curved through the air to land on the side of the capsule, his gloved hands grasping for a grip on the raised lips of a porthole ledge.

He clung fast for dear life as the capsule blew through the top of the museum in an explosion of timber and shingles. Then they were streaking upward into the starry night sky.

CHAPTER
2

Inside the capsule, Batman was thrown to the floor by the unexpected powerful acceleration. But, protected by the mechanisms built into his ingenious cryo-suit, Freeze stayed upright.

"You were a great scientist once," Batman reminded the villain as he struggled to rise. "Don't waste your genius on evil."

"I hate being lectured," Freeze snarled. He bent down and grabbed Batman. Muscles strained as he lifted the crimefighter and hurled him hard. Batman's back slammed painfully against the bulkhead. Before he could recover, Freeze had used his gun to freeze the hero's ankles and wrists to the metal wall in chunks of ice.

"Watch the numbers, Batman. For they are harbingers of your doom."

Batman glanced toward the capsule's altimeter, its

numerals whirling rapidly. Ten thousand feet — and rising.

"Can you feel it coming?" Freeze went on. "The icy cold of space. At thirty thousand feet your heart will freeze and beat no more."

As the numbers rolled grimly on to 15,000, Robin was struggling to climb up onto the capsule's nose cone. He had clamped twin potent bat-shaped magnets to the pod's steel side, and he made his way hand over hand, fighting against the fierce acceleration.

Inside the capsule, Batman was completely helpless as Freeze stepped into a glide-wing backpack mounted on the wall.

"After you have frozen," the villain sneered, "your icy tomb will fall back down on Gotham."

"You're mad, Freeze!" Batman snapped. "This capsule could slaughter thousands when it lands!"

Freeze hauled open the door in the capsule's side. Outside, the sky whipped past. "Ain't it grand?" He laughed. "Freeze well!"

He jumped out into the night and began to plummet toward the lights of Gotham City, twinkling far below.

Eighteen thousand feet. The air was thin and cold here, and the capsule was whiting over with hoary frost. Robin gasped for breath as he finally managed to yank off the hatch. Quickly, he dropped inside, where Batman was struggling to break his icy cuffs.

"I thought you were going to stay in the museum and round up the thugs," Batman greeted his partner.

"How about, 'Nice to see you'?" Robin replied, pulling a laser from his Utility Belt. "Or even, 'Glad you're here to save my life'?" A thin beam of intense heat flared from the small device, flash-melting one of the shackles on Batman's wrist.

"When we get home, we're having a little communication workshop," the older man said as Robin melted the other cuffs.

The altimeter read 20,000 feet and rising. Ice was forming everywhere now, coating the capsule interior under a heavy blanket of frost.

Batman whipped a bat-shaped charge from his belt, and hurled it to embed in the ceiling. "We have to make sure this rocket doesn't turn Gotham into a crater," he said curtly. A light on the Bat-charge flashed green. It was armed.

"Now what?" Robin asked lightly. "We call a taxi?"

For reply, Batman grabbed a handle marked CAUTION, EXPLOSIVE BOLTS. Immediately, Robin grasped his partner's intent. These were escape hatches. Robin gripped the ones on the capsule's far side.

They pulled the release handles together. The bolts blew with a loud crack, jettisoning the capsule doors outward. Still clinging on to the handles, Batman and Robin leaped out on the doors as they were blasted into space.

The light on the Bat-charge flashed red.

Perfectly balanced, like surfers about to hit the Big Wave, Batman and Robin skyboarded on the doors, spiraling downward, away from the capsule.

Seconds later, it exploded above them in a blaze of light, blown to smithereens by the charge's powerful explosive. Small pieces of debris fell toward them in flaming streamers as they surfed down.

Beneath them, they could just make out the figure of Mr. Freeze, the glide wing on his backpack allowing him to control his long, looping flight back to the city below.

Following in the villain's wake, Batman and Robin leveled out. They swayed and twisted, avoiding skyscrapers and elevated bridges as they continued to close on the fleeing crook.

Freeze didn't even know they were behind him until Batman swooped in. Pushing off from his skyboard door,

Batman grabbed Freeze around the neck. The diamond dropped from the thief's hand, and Robin flipped acrobatically to catch it.

Unable to shake Batman off, Freeze slapped the buckle of his glide pack in desperation. The catch released, the straps came free, and Batman and the glide pack spun away from him.

By the time Batman had dropped the pack and somersaulted into a rushing drop, Freeze was descending fast toward the giant smoking chimney of a towering industrial complex. He aimed his cryo-gun at the smoking tower below him, and fired. The blue beam literally sucked heat from everything it touched.

Unbelievably quickly, the vast maw of the chimney covered with snow and ice.

Freeze dropped into it dead center, firing his gun in measured bursts as he fell, slowing his descent by turning the chimney's insides into a madly snaking tunnel of ice before him.

Batman and Robin dropped into the ice shaft after him, only seconds behind. They plunged headfirst through layers of snow and frost. Pulling their grappling guns, they fired as one. The grapples bit deep into the chimney's brick lining, and held, slowing their crazy fall.

They landed at the start of a long, submarine-like corridor, in an industrial basement that looked like bleak Antarctica.

"Cool," Robin enthused. "Can we do that again?"

At the terminus of the tunnel lay a boiler room. Despite the heat that had pumped from it only minutes earlier, its internal reservoir was now frozen solid. In its center stood the massive boiler itself, its fiery warmth extinguished by Freeze's cryogenic mastery. It dripped ice.

As Batman pushed open the door to the room, Mr. Freeze leaped from behind it, slamming the metal portal hard in Batman's face. Batman stumbled forward, sagging, nearly unconscious from the ferocious blow. But even as Freeze raised his gun for the death stroke, a third figure joined the fray.

Without regard for his own safety, Robin dived toward the villain. Freeze turned and fired, and the daredevil didn't stand a chance of dodging. He caught the full force of the freeze gun's beam. Instantly, Robin turned into a frozen sculpture of ice.

Batman recovered his senses, staring in horror at his frozen partner. Dimly, he was aware of a rumbling far beneath his feet. Something tunneling through the earth — getting closer.

The rumble became a deafening roar — then suddenly the wall exploded in a harsh whine of spinning metal and pulverized brick. Another of Freeze's drilling trucks was visible in the clearing smoke, its automatic controls bringing it to its maker's side like a dog coming to its master.

"Can you be so cold, Batman?" the villain teased. "You have eleven minutes to thaw the bird. What will you do — chase the villain, or save the boy?"

Mr. Freeze leaped onto the huge vehicle. "Your emotions make you weak. That is why this day is mine." He smiled, chillingly, no trace of humor in his voice. "Stay cool, Bats."

In a roar of turbines, he was gone. The massive machine sealed the tunnel behind him with a blast of ice. There would be no pursuit.

Eleven minutes, Batman thought. The maximum time a body might stay alive before the freezing caused permanent and irreversible damage.

Batman moved swiftly to his partner's side, and brushed his finger against the boy's icy skin. He whipped out his belt laser and pointed it at the frozen reservoir.

The slim beam ate into the ice like a hot wire through butter, discharging massive amounts of energy into the frozen water. Within minutes, it was all melted. A minute more and it started to simmer.

Batman grabbed Robin and eased him to the edge of the

now-steaming water. Quickly, he immersed his unmoving partner in the reservoir, its warmth penetrating and melting Robin's flash-frozen flesh.

For one dreadful instant, Batman caught his breath. Was it going to work? Or was Robin . . . ?

Then his partner's head broke the surface. Coughing and spluttering, he looked up at his mentor and grinned weakly. "Did we get him?" he breathed.

CHAPTER

3

Deep in the South American rain forest, a heavy storm lashed the night. Thunder rolled ominously across the darkened skies, and jagged flashes of lightning illuminated a maze of tents and tarpaulins affixed to the decaying ruins of an ancient prison.

Inside one of the tents, a greenhouse laboratory had been set up. Bunsen burners flickered and beakers bubbled as Dr. Pamela Isley recorded the results of her experiments. "I still have high hopes for the animal-plant crossbreedings," she said into her small, cylindrical tape recorder.

She surveyed the two lab tables before her, brushing a strand of her mousy, lackluster hair from a pretty face obscured by heavy, unfashionable glasses. One table was covered in a mass of different plants. The other held dozens of tanks containing spiders, snakes, and scorpions. Delicate tubes ran from the poisonous beasts into a jar of strange, milky fluid. It was labeled VENOM. More tubes ran from the Venom jar into the plants, one of which was twitching and swaying as it received a dose of toxins.

"If only I can find the correct dose of Venom," Pamela continued into her recorder, "these plants will be able to defend themselves like animals. They'll be able to fight back. I will have given flora a chance against the thoughtless ravages of man."

Her blood ran cold as an agonized scream came from behind the solid prison wall against which her tent was pitched. Terrified, Pamela walked toward the source of the wail, a gothic prison door with PROJECT GILGAMESH stenciled on it.

"Personal note," she dictated. "My work would proceed faster if Dr. Woodrue didn't always whisk my Venom samples back to his mysterious Gilgamesh Wing. Why won't he let me into his lab?"

As if in reply, another bloodcurdling scream rent the night. Unexpectedly, the door opened. Startled, Pamela dropped the miniature recorder to the floor and stood transfixed. Her boss, Dr. Jason Woodrue, was framed in the doorway. His unruly white hair stood out in all directions, his cold eyes expressionless and emotionless. *Like a lizard,* Pamela couldn't help thinking.

"Dr. Isley — loveliest flower in our garden," Woodrue said. Even when paying a compliment, there was a hint of menace in the man's voice. "How fare our little wards?" He glanced down at the bottle of Venom, and reached to lift it in his hand. "What do we have here? A lovely new supply of Venom. I'll just take it to my lab for further study."

"What exactly are you doing in there?" Pamela asked. "What are those screams?"

Woodrue was illuminated by a fierce flash of lightning. "How I'd love to share my secrets with you," he said. "But I ask you, sweet sapling — can you be trusted? You refuse my invitations to dine. You hide yourself behind these sallow robes."

Pamela backed away from him. She was very happy in her "sallow robes," thank you.

A deafening clap of thunder seemed to shake the very earth. "Ah, but there's romance in the air tonight." Woodrue cackled. "Perhaps a moonlit stroll in the jungle, my dear?"

Pamela winced. There was nothing she'd like less. "You have to tell me what you're doing with my Venom," she said doggedly.

Woodrue's reply was sour. "You must show me *your* secrets, blossom, before I show you *mine*."

Pamela watched in silence as he turned to leave. As the door to the Gilgamesh Wing began to swing closed behind him, Pamela kicked her fallen recorder. The metal cylinder rolled across the floor and wedged itself between door and jamb, preventing the entrance from sealing.

She gave Woodrue a few seconds' start before she slipped through the doorway after him. She found herself in the main hallway of the long-abandoned prison and made her way along it, following the sound of the screams as they grew ever louder.

Dim light shone from a large chamber which Woodrue had converted into his Gilgamesh laboratory. Inside stood banks of flashing Cray supercomputers, connected up to a vast array of sparking, humming, high-tech equipment. Woodrue stood in shadows, a mobile phone in his hand.

"Ladies and gentlemen of the un-United Nations," he began, then said into the phone: "And our mystery bidder."

Careful not to make a sound, Pamela crouched behind the door. She could see that a small bridge arced across the room, with four distinct shapes standing on it. An American general, a Russian commissar, and an Arab sheik stood there, next to a man she recognized from news bulletins: he was the brutal dictator of a South American country.

"I give you the future of military conquest," Woodrue announced grandly.

A door in the far wall opened, and several gun-toting foot soldiers dragged a scrawny prisoner in a too-large tank suit into the room. Quickly, efficiently, the guards shackled him to a gurney. His shaven skull was adorned with three surgically implanted ducts.

"May I present Antonio Diego, serial murderer serving life in prison — and sole surviving volunteer." Woodrue broke off as Diego spat harshly at the last word. "And what a charmer he is!"

Every eye was on the prisoner, and Pamela took the opportunity to slip into the room, hiding herself behind a large stack of circuit boxes. She watched with a mixture of horror and growing understanding as Woodrue held up the jar of milky Venom.

"My super-soldier serum," he was saying. "Code named Venom. Patent pending, of course."

Swiftly, Woodrue poured the Venom into a state-of-the-art injector pack strapped to the back of the gurney. He lifted an open-front black-and-white mask attached by snaking tubes to the injector pack.

"Note the hassle-free zipper." Woodrue pulled the oversize mask over Diego's head. The tubes fitted directly and neatly into the ducts in the prisoner's skull. Woodrue zipped the fabric closed over the man's face, then hit a button on a remote control device.

Immediately the injector pack began to pump Venom into Diego's skull. Face hidden by the mask, Diego screamed, his body arching with pain; but the shackles pulled him back onto the gurney.

Her eyes widening with horror, hardly daring to breathe, Pamela watched as something incredible began to happen. Diego's body seemed to pulsate, as if it was swelling. His chest enlarged. His neck thickened, and his forearms grew. Every muscle rippled and bulged.

"Behold — the ideal killing machine," Woodrue said with pride in his voice. "I call him . . . Bane. Bane of humanity." He looked up at the audience on the small bridge. "Imagine it — your own personal army made up of thousands of these super-soldiers." He paused for effect. "Bidding begins at a mere ten million."

Woodrue hit the remote button again, upping the flow of the milky drug to Bane's mask. Impossibly, the prisoner grew even larger. His arm muscles strained, tendons standing out — and suddenly his shackles snapped. Pamela gave a silent gasp as the leg restraints quickly followed. Growling like an animal in pain, Bane lurched off the gurney and reached toward the Venom pump. His wildly thrashing hand struck a console and electric sparks fizzed and crackled.

Pamela screamed as spitting electrical components rained down around her. The foot soldiers rushed to subdue Bane, while Woodrue strode to the source of the scream.

"Welcome to my parlor," he snapped, and grabbed her by the arm.

Propelled along by his superior strength, Pamela was

hustled back out into the main hall. He marched her toward the door that gave access to her own tent lab, hissing out his explanation as they walked. "Our original sponsor had no stomach for military applications. So he cut the funding for our work —"

"*Our* work?" Pamela broke in.

Woodrue smiled. "Without your research I could never have come this far." He thought for a moment, then he offered, "Join me. The two of us, entwined, side by side . . ." They had reached the door of her workshop, and Woodrue shoved her through it.

"Join you?" Pamela said bitterly. "I've spent my life trying to protect plants from extinction, and now you corrupt my research into some maniacal scheme for world domination!" She gave a derisive snort. "When I get through, you won't be able to get a job teaching high school chemistry. Do you hear me, you psycho?"

"Well, I can respect your opinion," Woodrue said nonchalantly, then pushed Pamela viciously backward into the interconnected lab tables. They collapsed under her weight and she fell to the floor, buried in an avalanche of plants and poisonous insects as they slid off the table onto her.

"I'm not good at rejection," Woodrue said. He grasped hold of a shelf of specimen jars and yanked hard. The whole unit fell on top of Pamela. Strange, bubbling liquids splashed from beakers. A dozen kinds of poisonous insects swarmed across her body, biting and nipping and ripping at her flesh.

Coldly, clinically, Woodrue pulled over another shelf. This time poisonous plant extracts from foxglove and jimson weed and a dozen different ivies spilled over her. "I'm afraid you'll have to die."

Pamela whimpered in pain, struggling to get up. But another heavy shelf crashed down on her head, and her movements ceased abruptly.

Woodrue smiled, and headed back into the prison hallway. "Fellow maniacs," he called out, "bidding begins!"

CHAPTER

4

In the depths of the Batcave, far below Wayne Manor, Dick Grayson — alias Robin — was recovering from his ordeal. He sat wrapped in a heavy blanket, a steaming mug of cocoa in his hand. Despite Batman's swift thaw, being frozen had left him with a bad case of the shivers.

Batman had slipped down his cowl, revealing the chiseled features of Gotham's most notorious playboy, the billionaire industrialist Bruce Wayne.

Robin watched as Batman flipped on the main monitor.

"Gotham University labs security video," Batman explained, and images scrolled onto the screen. "Two years ago."

The video showed the interior of a gleaming laboratory. A beautiful young woman, Nora Fries, lay on a gurney. Her scientist husband worked a bank of controls over a smoking vat of cryonic solution. He was a handsome man, his eyes reflecting the intense gaze of genius.

"Dr. Victor Fries." Batman gave a running commentary. "Two-time Olympic decathlete. Nobel Prize winner in molecular biology. After his wife contracted a rare disease, McGregor's Syndrome, he hoped to freeze her in cryogenic sleep until he could discover a cure."

On the screen, alarms flashed. A panel exploded next to Victor Fries, blowing him back into the vat of ultra-low-temperature solution. "That liquid is fifty below zero," Batman noted.

Fries was screaming, engulfed in the mists of the cryonic liquids. His skin froze, rapidly turning blue. His hair turned brittle, breaking off from his frozen scalp.

"That's gotta hurt!" Robin said through gritted teeth.

"Somehow he survived. But the cryogenic solution mutated his body."

"What happened to his wife?" Robin asked.

Batman shrugged. "Presumed dead. No one knows."

The screen image changed abruptly, to show a schematic of Mr. Freeze in his special cryo-suit. Compartments in both suit sleeves were highlighted, with flashing diamond shapes within.

"He needs extreme cold to survive," Batman explained. "His cryo-suit uses diamond-enhanced lasers to keep him at precisely zero degrees."

Robin shook his head slowly. "Let me get this straight — a brilliant citizen, disfigured by a horrible accident, reemerges as a psychotic supervillain bent on theft, revenge, and destruction." He glanced at Batman. "You see a pattern here?"

Batman knew Robin was referring to Harvey Dent, the dazzling district attorney who'd been scarred in an acid attack which drove him mad and turned him into the criminal Two-Face. "Maybe it's something in the water," Batman said, and returned his partner's smile.

Batman thought for a moment, then said, "Well, if it's ice the Iceman wants . . ." He turned to call out, "Alfred!"

In one of the costume vaults, Alfred Pennyworth stood clutching a console. His eyes were closed and his lips quivered as a wave of searing pain coursed through him. He waited till it passed, then straightened and regained his composure.

When he walked into the Batcave moments later, no one would ever have guessed there was anything wrong with him.

"I need the Wayne diamonds," Batman instructed.

Robin's eyes narrowed. "We gonna trap ourselves a snowman?" he asked.

"Absolutely," Batman replied. "Just as soon as you take ten hours' training on the simulator."

Robin's eyebrows shot up. "Whoa!" he protested. "I

made a mistake. I'm sorry. Don't go all protective on me. It won't happen again."

"You were reckless," Batman said with grim seriousness. "You could have been killed."

"I'm fine," the young man shot back. He gestured to himself with one hand. "See — me. Here. Alive. How are we ever gonna work together if you're never gonna trust me?"

"How indeed?" Alfred broke in.

Batman stared at the two of them, then gave a wry smile. "When did I become the bad guy?" he asked.

Five minutes later, Bruce Wayne and Alfred walked together up the steps leading from the Batcave to the elegant mansion above. "Dick's overeager, impulsive," Bruce was saying. "I can't trust him not to get hurt."

"Perhaps the truth is you don't really trust anyone," Alfred said in measured tones.

"Don't tell me you're on his side. Again."

"Despite all your talents, you are still a novice in the ways of family," Alfred said sagely. "Master Dick follows the same star as you, but gets there by his own course. You must learn to trust him. For that is the nature of family."

Bruce knew the old butler was right. Alfred had cared for him ever since that awful childhood night when his parents were gunned down before his terrified eyes. The man had never lied to him, had always steered him straight. Bruce looked deep into his eyes.

"I trust *you,* Alfred," he said simply.

Alfred seemed oddly pained by Bruce's words. But all he said was: "I shan't be here forever, sir."

Bruce waited for him to say more, but the butler just smiled and murmured, "Good night."

Alone in his quarters, Alfred booted up his computer. He slipped a compact disc into the drive and began to type.

"Override engaged," the computer announced in a tinny voice. "Copying protected files."

Alfred lifted a microrecorder and began to speak into it. "I am still unable to reach you. I have vital information which you must see."

On-screen, the files Alfred was copying flashed and scrolled. The Batmobile design. The Batman costume schematics. The Utility Belt. Plans of the Batcave. Every secret of the Batman that Alfred knew was being down-loaded onto the wafer-thin disc.

The storm had passed, and a full moon shone down on the abandoned South American prison. Inside, Jason

Woodrue stood at Pamela Isley's workstation, riffling through her voluminous research notes as he spoke into his mobile phone.

"Yes, sir, I'm so pleased you won the bidding, your supreme ruthlessness." He paused as Bane screamed in the distance. "We're making the final modifications to Bane right now. We'll have a thousand super-soldiers out to you tomorrow by overnight mail."

He flicked the phone off. For a moment there was perfect silence. Then — a rustling. Woodrue frowned, and squinted at a patch of ivy. Before he could even move, a figure burst from beneath the vegetation.

A woman stood before him, magenta hair gleaming in the moonlight. Her eyes blazed chlorophyll-green. Her ravaged clothes revealed the form and bearing of a goddess. Woodrue gaped.

"Dr. Isley?" He frowned. "Pamela? You look great. Especially for a dead woman."

The woman who had once been Pamela Isley moved toward him. "Hello, Jason," she said huskily, her voice low and sensuous. "I think I've had a change of heart."

Stunned by her beauty, Woodrue didn't attempt to move away as she leaned forward and kissed him delicately on the lips. "Quite literally had a change of heart," she went on. "I don't think I'm human anymore. The animal-plant toxins seem to have had rather a unique effect on me."

Woodrue felt suddenly light-headed. He heard Pamela's words as if through a tank of water: "They replaced my blood with aloe and chlorophyll . . . and filled my lips with Venom."

Suddenly a bolt of pain stabbed through Woodrue. He gasped, began to choke, and fell to the floor, clutching at his throat.

"I probably should have mentioned this earlier," Pamela told him. "I'm poison. Poison Ivy." She shrugged expressively. "It's a jungle in here."

She reached out and sent a shelf of chemical beakers crashing to the floor. Casually, she tossed a flaming Bunsen burner on top of the spill, and sudden flames erupted.

"Let the flames touch the sky," Poison Ivy intoned, but Jason Woodrue could no longer hear her. He was dead. "For I am Nature's arm, her spirit, her will. The time has come for plants to take back the world so rightfully ours. Because it's not nice to fool with Mother Nature."

A reflection caught her eye. She bent to pick up a broken beaker. On it, the easily recognizable logo of Wayne Enterprises was clearly visible. So that's who'd been funding them.

Ivy frowned at the sound of Bane's distant scream. The

flames were spreading; she could leave the monster Woodrue had created to perish in the fire. But . . . Bane might have other uses.

Poison Ivy turned and walked into the prison hall. "Coming, Bane," she called sweetly. "We've got a plane to catch!"

CHAPTER

5

A pale moon shone down on the long-abandoned Snowy Cones Ice Cream Factory. In its time, it had been one of the strangest buildings in all of Gotham City, built in the shape of a giant snowman's face. To complete the image, a huge dripping ice cream cone was stuck onto the massive snowball head.

Inside, snow covered every surface. Ice sculptures stood in a dozen locations. Rime hung in the air. This was Mr. Freeze's secret hideout.

In the monument to cold, Mr. Freeze paced like a trapped animal.

"To be frozen," he was muttering to himself, "to never change. A life of perpetual *ice*-olation. There is no perfection in that."

A display on his cryo-suit began to flash: LOW POWER. Battling the Batman had exhausted his energy supply, and there was only one way to replenish it. He took three small diamonds from a safe and placed them carefully in the suit compartment. At once his power levels spiked to normal.

Atop a pedestal sat a strange machine. Niches in it held two giant diamonds — its power supply. But slots for two more diamonds stood empty. Freeze pulled out the giant gem he'd stolen from the museum — the Second Sun of the Sudan — and placed it in one of the vacant slots.

One more giant diamond and his Freezing Cannon would be complete. He intended to hold the entire city hostage with it, turning Gotham into eternal winter unless his demands were met. The city fathers would have no choice but to give him the billions of dollars he required to complete his research. *And find the cure for Nora,* Freeze thought sadly.

He headed into a large walk-in freezer stuffed with packages and cans of frozen food. He went directly to a certain frozen dinner box and lifted it, setting a secret mechanism in motion. Part of the wall slid back, revealing a spacious hidden vault.

Within, a computerized, glacierlike holding tank contained a female figure. Nora Fries. His wife. Frozen in suspended animation until he could find a cure for the awful disease that had ravaged her. Light sparkled off the snowflake pendant she wore around her neck. The pendant he'd once given her, to declare his eternal love.

Tenderly, the villain leaned to touch the glass. "Soon we will be together once more," he whispered.

Columns of dancing sunbeams filled the impressive entryway to Wayne Manor. It was the next afternoon, and the insistent ringing of the doorbell prompted Dick Grayson to answer it himself.

Dick opened the heavy oak front door as Bruce came down the staircase and met Alfred. The butler emerged from the direction of the kitchen. "I must have dozed off," Alfred said, somewhat embarrassed. "My sincerest apologies, sir."

Bruce shook his head. "No apology necessary. That's the first time in thirty years."

He smiled, but behind the smile there was concern. Alfred seemed pale, frailer than usual.

"Mystery pizza delivery?" Dick greeted the caller as he stuck his head around the carved door.

A young girl stood there, beautiful in the golden light. Her pretty face seemed to shine with an inner glow, and though she was dressed in prim schoolgirl clothes, Dick felt his heart skip a beat.

"Please be looking for me," he almost drooled.

The girl looked up shyly and saw Alfred standing

with Bruce. The old man's eyes widened as he caught sight of her.

"Uncle Alfred?" the girl cried. She rushed in past Dick and Bruce and threw herself into the old butler's arms. Alfred's face lit up with joy as he hugged her close.

Bruce and Dick exchanged bewildered glances. "'Uncle?'" both mouthed at the same time.

The girl's name was Barbara Wilson, and a little later, as they showed her around the Wayne estate's magnificent gardens, Alfred explained all.

"She isn't really my niece," he told Bruce and Dick, who could hardly take his eyes off the girl. "She's Margaret Clark's daughter."

Alfred had fallen in love with Margaret while he'd been visiting Metropolis many years earlier. But she was twenty years younger than he. When he realized the age difference would be unfair to her, he returned to Gotham. Margaret had married a young physician on the rebound, and Barbara was their daughter.

The quartet walked up a flight of stone steps flanked by dazzling blooms, past a pool where a small fountain burbled. "Is your mother here, too?" Dick asked — and knew immediately that he shouldn't have, by the looks on the others' faces.

"My parents were killed in an auto accident ten years ago," Barbara said sadly. But she cheered almost at once as she squeezed Alfred's arm. "Alfred has been supporting me ever since."

Bruce was surprised. "You have, Alfred?"

The old man smiled wryly. "Secrets are a virtual prerequisite in this house, don't you think, sir?"

They followed the path that curved across the lawns and led to the garages at the side of the house.

Barbara lived in England, where she was a computer science major at the ancient Oxbridge Academy. She was telling them how she'd had a sudden whim to visit Alfred during her term break when she stopped, staring. Dick followed her gaze to the motorcycle that sat gleaming in the afternoon sunshine.

"What is it?" she asked. "It's . . . beautiful."

"A competition racer I've been fixing up," Dick told her. "Maybe one day I'll show you how to ride it."

"You certainly will not," Alfred said sternly, and Barbara agreed.

"Oh no, those things frighten me."

Dick couldn't be sure, but he thought she didn't sound a hundred percent sincere about that.

"I hope you'll be staying with us," Bruce invited.

"All this luxury isn't really my style," Barbara admitted. She gazed again at the bike. "But I'd love to stay."

Alfred looked unsure. "Oh, but Master Bruce," he protested. "So much goes on —"

"Don't be silly, Alfred," Bruce said airily. "After all, she's family."

In the vaults concealed in the Snowy Cones factory, Mr. Freeze had labored all day. Now he stood at his computer workstation, punching in data.

"Perhaps this time," he said softly, hitting a switch, "the new formula will return you to me."

He glanced at his wife. *So beautiful,* he thought. *So unfair that you should be trapped like this. But perhaps this time —*

His thoughts broke off. The ALERT panel was flashing its simple message: TEST FAILURE. Anguish showed on Freeze's face, and his angry fist came smashing down on the console.

"No cure tonight, love," he whispered to his frozen wife. "Forgive me. But soon, I promise you. Soon."

Barbara Wilson tapped on Alfred's bedroom door. No reply. She gathered her long terry bathrobe around her, pushed the door open, and entered.

"Uncle Alfred?"

The room appeared to be empty. Barbara saw the pile of envelopes stacked on the desk, and looked closer. All were addressed to Wilfred Pennyworth, Royal Court of Mirajanpore. Every single one was stamped RETURN TO SENDER.

"I didn't know sneaking around was on the curriculum at Oxbridge."

Barbara started at the butler's voice behind her. Alfred stepped from the shadows, wearing a robe.

"I'm sorry, Uncle. I came to tuck you in . . ."

"*You* came to tuck *me* in? That's quite a switch." Alfred looked toward the heap of envelopes. "I am looking for my brother, Wilfred," he explained. "He is first butler to the Maharajah of Mirajanpore. But Mirajanpore is a floating court, traveling the length and breadth of India, so Wilfred can be rather difficult to find."

"I guess they don't have fax machines on elephants," Barbara said with a smile. Looking around the room, she saw a framed photograph on the desk. The image of a lovely woman's face bore the inscription "*All my love. Peg.*" Barbara had placed that same photo of her mother by the bed in her room at Oxbridge. But "Peg"?

"My nickname for Margaret," Alfred told her, eyes misty with memory. "The heart often finds its own language."

Barbara smiled affectionately. "I've missed you, Uncle Alfred."

"As I've missed you." The old man planted a gentle kiss on her forehead. "Good night now. Sleep well."

Barbara made her way back along the oak-paneled corridor to her room. She waited for the light to go out under Alfred's door, then slipped inside. Closing the door behind her, Barbara whipped off her bulky robe — to reveal that she was wearing a tight black leather motorcycle outfit underneath. She pulled on a pair of sleek black boots.

Seconds later, she was lowering herself from the bedroom balcony on the end of a knotted climbing rope. She'd memorized the layout of the grounds during the tour earlier, and was able to head directly for the vast underground garage that housed Bruce Wayne's collection of exotic cars.

At the far end, beyond the gleaming bodies of some of the world's most expensive vehicles, was a row of motorcycles. Barbara's eye fell on the sleek competition racer. Dick's pride and joy. Pulling a helmet from her backpack, she climbed onto the powerful machine and expertly kickstarted the engine.

She kept the throttle low until she was well away from the house, heading down the sweeping drive. Then she opened it up, and the engine wailed as she surged forward into the night.

CHAPTER

6

Next morning, a dark limousine pulled away from Gotham Airport and headed for the city. At the wheel, barely disguised by the bulky chauffeur's uniform he wore, was Bane. In the backseat, Poison Ivy underwent a startling transformation. She applied brown contact lenses to her eyes, and donned a dark wig. Her expression lost its malevolent mischief, and went back to just plain frumpy.

Poison Ivy became Pamela Isley once more.

The Gotham Observatory stood high atop the steep banks of the Gotham River, towering over the city far below. A vast stone and copper building, it had fallen into disrepair in recent years, but was now being restored. Its huge dome had been relined, and one of the biggest telescopes in the Western world had been installed.

A crowd of reporters and hangers-on was gathered in the

immense circular hall, still under construction, where the telescope was mounted. A viewing platform stood at its end, and a circular balcony ran around the inside of the dome.

Bruce Wayne was standing on a small podium, flanked by his date, the beautiful Julie Madison, and several scientists. The gaggle of TV and newspaper reporters faced them.

"My father once told me," Bruce began, addressing the throng, "that to succeed we need only pick our star and follow it. And so Wayne Enterprises is donating the world's most advanced telescope to Gotham's Observatory Restoration Project. Perhaps this telescope will give future generations a chance to find their own stars."

"Is it true this telescope can see all around the globe?" a newsman called out.

One of the scientists answered. "Yes. If you'll watch the monitors —" A bank of screens came to life with images. A graphic of planet Earth. Diagrams of equidistant satellites in geosynchronous orbit. "Satellites already in orbit allow us to reflect light around the globe," the scientist went on. He paused as the graphic ray of light on-screen was reflected from a satellite over Australia, to one over America, and then beamed to a graphic of the Gotham telescope. "From here we'll be able to see the sky anywhere on earth."

But as usual, the journalists were soon bored with technicalities. For them, the real news was billionaire Bruce Wayne's romance.

"Brucie, you and the exquisite Julie Madison have been going out for, oh, months now," Gossip Gerty, the city's most popular columnist, called out. "Are you planning to tie the knot?"

Bruce hoped his expression was suitably surprised. "Married? Me? Good heavens, no!"

Julie glared at him. Flustered, he quickly backtracked. "Umm, what I mean is . . . no plans at the moment."

It suited Bruce to have a girlfriend like Julie. She asked no questions about his nocturnal excursions, and was always ready to drop everything to attend a party or social event with him. She was good camouflage for his role as Batman. It was easy to forget that although he was playing a role, Julie Madison was not.

But like the well-bred girl she was, Julie was in control of the situation. She turned to the flashing cameras. "Bruce and I are lucky enough to be in love. That is most certainly enough for us." She glanced at Bruce, and added under her breath: "For now."

The scientist called for attention, and led the pack off toward the central control grid. As Bruce hung back, a security guard approached him.

"Mr. Wayne?" The guard pointed to a frumpy figure, her

hair pulled back in a severe bun, eyes lost behind ugly glasses. "She doesn't have a pass, sir."

Bruce smiled and waved the man off. "You're not going to hurt me, are you, Ms . . . ?"

"Doctor. Dr. Pamela Isley."

"What can I do for you, doctor? A research grant? A hospital wing?" Bruce said magnanimously.

Pamela didn't smile. "Actually, I already work for you. Or did," she corrected herself. "Your arboreal preservation project in South America."

Bruce frowned. "We cut off support. A conflict of ideologies. To be blunt, Jason Woodrue was a lunatic." Bruce thought for a moment. "I heard that lab was consumed by fire last week. You managed to escape?"

Pamela ignored his question. She thrust out a document. "I have here a proposal showing how Wayne Enterprises can immediately cease all actions that toxify our environment."

Bruce took it, intrigued, and scanned it quickly. Pamela's eyes shone as she went on: "Forget the stars. Look here, at the Earth, our mother. She deserves our loyalty and protection. And yet you spoil her lands, poison her oceans, blacken her skies. You're killing her," she finished accusingly.

"Your intentions are noble, Dr. Isley," Bruce remarked.

"But no fossil fuel for heat? No coolants to preserve food? Millions would die of cold and hunger alone."

"Acceptable losses in a battle to save the planet."

"People come first, doctor," Bruce said icily. He handed back the document.

As the scientist led the group back toward them, Pamela indicated them with contempt. "Mammals! So smug in your towers of stone and glass. A day of reckoning is coming! The same plants and flowers that saw you crawl blindly from the primordial soup will reclaim this world," she ranted on, warming to her theme. "Earth will be a garden again! Somehow, some way, I will bring your man-made civilization to its knees — and there will be no one there to protect you!"

Her tirade was so extreme, several people laughed out loud. "You must be new in town," a veteran reporter said. "In Gotham City, Batman and Robin protect us. Even from plants and flowers!"

"Perhaps you'd like to meet them," Bruce offered, in an attempt to prevent the situation from escalating. He nodded to an aide, and the man stepped forward holding out an invitation card.

"'Batman and Robin to appear at the Flower Ball,'" Pamela read.

"They're helping us auction off a prized diamond to

raise money for the Gotham Botanical Gardens. Just a few mammals doing what we can for the world's plants." Bruce gave a little bow. "Although the Wayne Foundation is hosting the event, I will sadly be unable to attend. Thank you all. Good day, Dr. Isley."

Pamela watched Bruce's retreating back for a moment, then frowned at her invitation. "Batman and Robin," she hissed. "Militant arm of the warm-blooded oppressors! Animal protectors of the status quo! First I'll rid myself of the winged and feathered pests — and then Gotham will be mine for the greening!"

The Flower Ball, one of Gotham's prime social events of the year, was held at the Botanical Gardens. The gardens were enclosed in an immense glass greenhouse set atop the roof of a mighty skyscraper. Elegant guests milled and mingled amid tropical greenery under the stars, while only yards away elevated highways snaked past.

A giant beast mask covered the entrance to the ball. Inside, a troupe of drummers pounded an exotic rhythm on their congas. A couple dressed as gorillas romped around, amusing the guests. Many of them were dressed as flowers, or in outfits richly decorated with floral themes.

Batman and Robin stood in the shadows near the stage. They preferred it when the public wasn't aware of their presence, but sometimes it couldn't be helped. Like tonight.

"You think Freeze will take the bait?" Robin wanted to know.

Batman was adamant. "He'll be here." He knew there were few diamonds of the necessary size and purity to power Freeze's sophisticated equipment. It had been in all the papers and news broadcasts that the Wayne gems would be at the Flower Ball. There was no chance Freeze wouldn't show.

Atop the stairs, the two prancing gorillas converged on the conga drummers. One danced around, covertly knocking the drummers unconscious with his heavy paws.

The master of ceremonies walked out onto the stage, accompanied by Gossip Gerty. After the emcee had welcomed the guests, two armed guards emerged bearing a cushioned velvet pallet. On it hung a silver necklace supporting a perfect diamond.

"The famed Heart of Isis," Gossip Gerty announced, "on loan from the personal collection of my close friend Bruce Wayne."

The emcee gestured and several women stepped forward. Each was dressed as a different variety of flower, and each was more gorgeous than the next. "Tonight, on auction," he announced to the excited guests, "an opportunity to dine with one of our fabulous flowers, the famed Heart of Isis draped around her neck."

A stout man held up a hand. "I bid ten thousand dollars for Chrysanthemum!"

"Twenty for Lilac!"

"Thirty for Rose!"

At the top of the stairs, during the commotion of the auction, all of the drummers had been knocked out and their bodies dragged off. Now one of the gorillas began to beat the drums, while the other removed her paw mitts. She reached up to peel off the headmask, and from the unzipped costume stepped forth a vision. Poison Ivy, in a costume of skintight green, with boots and mask, looked almost impossibly beautiful.

Ivy lifted her green-gloved hands, which were filled with piles of sparkling dust. Before anyone thought to stop her, she blew and scattered the powder over the surprised throng. The dust spun out in fairylike spirals, curling through the crowd.

Guests blinked, suddenly bewitched by the blend of plant-based chemicals she'd used to create the hypnotic Love Dust. With no reason to be suspicious, Batman and Robin inhaled the potent dust as well.

Ivy sauntered casually toward them, ignoring the entranced men who watched her pass.

"Hi there." She reached out a hand to Batman, who stood dazed, his normally keen mind fuddled by the dust's effects. "I like a man in black."

Batman could only gape at her, knowing how foolish he must look but unable to prevent himself. Ivy turned away from him, to Robin. "Of course," she purred, "youth does have its advantages."

Robin stared at her, his eyes huge. She was the most beautiful woman he'd ever seen. He couldn't think of anything else. He didn't want to think of anything else.

Ivy vaulted up onto the stage and took the microphone from the mesmerized emcee. Then she lifted the Heart of Isis from its pallet and hung it around her neck.

"Some lucky man gets dinner with Poison Ivy. Who'll start the bidding?" she asked sweetly.

There was an immediate chorus from the crowd. "A hundred thousand for Poison Ivy!"

Despite himself, Batman called out, "One million!"

Robin shot him a dirty look, then turned back to the stage. "Two million!"

"You don't have two million," Batman hissed under his breath. Then, out loud: "Three million!"

"I'll borrow it from you," Robin whispered, before calling out, "Four million!"

Batman felt a sudden slight drop in temperature. Forcing himself to ignore the drug's effect, he tried to act rationally. Fighting his own feelings every inch of the way, he hauled a Batarang from his Utility Belt. From the corner of his eye, he could see Robin going through the same inner struggle as he pulled out a Throwing Bird.

Gossip Gerty gave a little shiver. "Is it getting nippy in here?" she asked.

Suddenly the giant entrance mask exploded as Mr. Freeze's truck leaped from an elevated highway, soared through the air, and smashed into the room. Freeze stood atop the vehicle, enveloped in swirling chill mists, his Icemen following behind.

"Did I use the wrong door again?" he said as he drew his cryo-gun.

Batman's Batarang sang through the air, careening into Freeze's hand and sending the gun spinning away. Both heroes raced forward, to be engulfed by the rushing swarm of Icemen.

As the gun arced down, one of the guests reached out to grab it. He'd scarcely held it a moment when an Iceman rammed into his back, sending the gun flying again.

A dozen security guards and as many guests rushed to swamp Freeze by sheer weight of numbers. "When technology fails," the villain muttered, "fall back on brute force."

He moved like lightning, fists flying in all directions, sending guests and experienced guards alike crashing across the room. Like a wildly fumbled football, his gun spun from guest to thug to guest again. Finally an Iceman sent the soaring gun tipping back toward Freeze. The villain dispatched another guard with a fearsome blow, reaching up to grab the weapon in his other hand.

"Everybody chill!" he snapped, beams of frigid potency ripping across the room. Three guests and several exotic flower arrangements turned instantly to ice.

"I should have been a decorator," Freeze remarked casually as he started for the stage.

Batman and Robin called on their entire repertoire of martial arts to fight off the army of Icemen. It always amazed Batman how easily crooks like Freeze could find thugs willing to take their dirty money. But he had no sympathy for them, as his feet and hands lashed out to land brutal, stunning blows. These men had chosen to do evil—they had no option but to accept the painful consequences.

Beside him, Robin fought like a demon, making up in speed what he lacked in body weight. A spinning side kick sent one thug flying, and a well-aimed elbow took out another.

Freeze climbed up onto the stage, to find himself face to face with Poison Ivy. "Let me guess," he sneered. "Plant Girl? Vine Lady? Ms. Moss?"

"Listen, Captain Cold," Ivy shot back scathingly, "the suit, maybe, even though silver went out in the seventies."

She gestured toward his feet, clad in heavy cryo-boots. "But those boots are unforgivable!"

Freeze held out a hand, expectant. "I'd love to stand here all night and exchange fashion tips, but I'm kind of pressed for time. So hand over the diamond, Garden Gal, or I'll turn you into frozen mulch!"

In reply, Ivy pulled a handful of her Love Dust from her belt pouch and blew it at him. The dust swirled around Freeze's helmet, but didn't penetrate. Ivy frowned, perplexed.

"Pheromone dust," Freeze guessed. "Designed to heat a man's blood. Doesn't work on the coldhearted, though. Now if you please —"

Poison Ivy held out the Heart of Isis diamond and dropped it into his gloved hand. "If you insist."

"Clever little clover," Freeze replied.

Just then one of Freeze's thugs sailed past them and smashed hard into the back of the stage. Batman and Robin were getting closer.

"That's my exit cue." Freeze turned and ran for his truck.

Batman and Robin finished dispatching the last of the Icemen, and vaulted onto the stage.

"You have eleven minutes to thaw those frozen people," Batman called to the unaffected guests. "Do it!"

As several men moved to comply, the heroes raced after the fleeing felon.

Poison Ivy stared after them. She bent to lift a small souvenir from a table. A glass globe with a miniature version of Gotham City inside it. She shook it, and suddenly the inside was full of swirling snowflakes.

A second gorilla appeared behind her. He pulled off his mask, revealing himself to be Bane.

"Enough monkey business," she told him. Her scheme had been totally upstaged by Mr. Freeze's daring heist. She would have to think of another plan. "We've got work to do."

CHAPTER
7

Mr. Freeze's customized ice truck raced through the midnight streets. Two cronies' trucks swayed along behind him, struggling to keep up with their boss. Horns blared and tires squealed as the speeding trucks hogged the road, forcing other traffic to swerve and skid to safety.

Ahead, rising from the skyscrapers like the Colossus of Gotham, stood a statue of gigantic proportions. The figure represented Mercury, the messenger of the gods, and an army of builders had labored for more than a year on its construction. Freeze steered his truck toward it, accelerating up the interconnecting bridges that crisscrossed the city skyline.

As the trucks roared ever higher, the road approaching ever closer to the statue's top, Freeze punched a flashing gun-shaped button on his dashboard. Atop his truck, a giant freeze-gun rose, its sights lining up on the statue's huge head. The gun fired abruptly, a beam of hyperintense cold shooting out from its barrel.

The statue's head froze as the beam hit it. For a moment, nothing happened as the effects of the cold were discharged throughout the stonework, turning its very molecules to ice. Then the neck of the gargantuan figure burst open in a frigid explosion.

Freeze stamped on the accelerator and wrenched the steering wheel violently. His truck veered off the road and sailed into the air. Its momentum carried it right through the hole in the statue's neck. The truck skidded briefly as Freeze brought it under control, then lurched down the statue's shoulder.

Behind, the two trucks followed. Their drivers swung the wheels this way and that, struggling to retain mastery as the three trucks sped down the statue's arm as if it were the biggest ski jump in the world.

Mere seconds behind the crooks and gaining all the time, the Batmobile and the Redbird were in hot pursuit. They leaped together from the highway, arcing down through the jagged hole in the statue's neck.

Inside the Batmobile, advanced electronics computed every possibility. The Freeze vehicles were obviously using the statue's arm as a ramp, intending to leap off from the fingers of its plaza-size hand. If they succeeded, if they made it to the lower roofs far beyond, their escape was virtually guaranteed.

Schematics flashed across Batman's screens. Potential trajectories of the three vehicles scrolled. Batman glanced in his side mirror, and saw the Redbird keeping pace with him.

"Pull back," he growled. "You can't make the jump."

"I can make it," Robin's voice crackled back, not a hint of doubt in his mind.

The Batmobile flew down the statue's arm. "Pull back!" Batman said again, his voice authoritative.

Bent low over the Redbird, the chill air whipping past him, Robin shook his head defiantly. "I can make it!"

Robin revved his throttle hard and the Redbird leaped forward, front wheel rising as it overtook the Batmobile. Under his cowl, Batman frowned. Robin was going to ignore him.

"Redbird control codes," Batman snapped, and the voice-activated computer responded at once. Blueprints and strings of code flashed on-screen. DISABLE ENGINE!

Robin readied himself for the jump ahead. He could see Freeze's trucks racing onto the hand, splitting up, going to use different fingers as their launch pads. He blinked in disbelief as the Redbird's warning light flared, and the mo-

tor began to fade. Cursing under his breath, he skidded to the side and grounded the bike.

At the same moment, Freeze's truck took off. Its superthrusters flamed into life, propelling it through the air, over the dizzying gap below. It seemed to hang there for an instant, as if suspended, and then it was over. Front wheels and chassis hit the low, sloping roof in a blaze of sparks. The truck righted itself, and spun around 180 degrees to face the way it had come.

Freeze's cronies weren't so skilled — or so lucky. Taking off from the finger ramps, the first one failed to gain the height it required. It arced down prematurely, and an orange fireball lit the night as it exploded into the wall of the opposite building.

The second truck made the height, but not the trajectory. It veered off at an angle, crashing into the neon lights of an elevated billboard before beginning its descent to the streets below.

The Redbird slid dangerously close to the edge, and Robin all but snarled in anger as the Batmobile shot past him, engine roaring, and rocketed into the air.

In the cab of his truck, Freeze gave an icy smile. "It's a cold town," he said, thumbing the gun-shaped dash button. The gun on top of his truck flared into life, its shimmering beam lancing out to envelop the soaring Batmobile.

Batman shivered as the windshield iced over in a flash. The SYSTEMS FAILURE warning began to flash on his monitor. Another few seconds and he'd be dead, iced forever!

Desperately, he forced his freezing limbs to react. Shaking with cold, his finger hit the EJECT button.

The windshield shattered in a thousand frozen shards as Batman was catapulted through it like a torpedo. He flipped over, warmth returning almost immediately to his body. His cape whipped open like the wings of some great, dark angel.

The ice sculpture that was the Batmobile soared on, to land safely on the rooftops, where it slowed and skidded to a halt.

Batman rode the urban winds, angling into a steep dive.

Below, Freeze thought he had escaped unscathed. He'd lost two trucks, and a dozen men — but so what? There were plenty more willing to fill the dead men's shoes, willing to risk their lives for the sky-high wages Freeze offered.

He looked up in surprise as the shadow of the Bat fell across the cab of his truck. Cape extended, Batman soared directly overhead, dropping fast. Before the villain could react, Batman smashed through the glass driver's dome, grabbed Freeze, and wrenched him out.

Batman's cape wings carried them on, swooping down toward a lower rooftop. Batman let Freeze go without warning, and the villain crashed down with stunning impact. The Dark Knight landed deftly beside him.

"I'm putting you on ice," he said. But Mr. Freeze didn't hear. He was out cold, the stolen Heart of Isis still clutched in his hand.

CHAPTER

8

Wayne Manor stood bathed in moonlight on its cliff-top perch above the gorge of the Gotham River. Deep beneath it, in the maze of tunnels and caverns that honeycombed the bedrock, its owner was engaged in an angry argument.

Batman had stripped off his costume and resumed his ordinary casual clothes, becoming Bruce Wayne again. Likewise, Robin had transformed back into plain Dick Grayson.

"I could have made the jump," Dick insisted for the tenth time, a hard edge to his voice.

"You could have splattered your brains on the side of the building," Bruce shot back.

They emerged from the costume vault and headed for the entrance together.

"You know," Dick went on, more reasonably, "in the circus the Flying Graysons were a team. We had to trust each person to do his part. That's what being partners is all about. Sometimes counting on someone else is the only way to win."

"Your mind wasn't even on the job," Bruce accused. "All you could think about was Poison Ivy!"

Dick shot his mentor a fierce glare. Bruce had touched a raw nerve. "You just can't stand that she might have wanted me instead of you," Dick snapped. "That's your idea of friendship, isn't it, Bruce? You have to have everything. Your house. Your rules. Your way or the highway." Even as he said the words, he knew he was being unfair. But somehow he still wasn't thinking straight. And besides, he reminded himself, Ivy *did* prefer him. "It's always Batman and Robin, never Robin and Batman. And I'm sick of it!"

They halted together, angry faces thrust close to each other. "Yes, it's my rules," Bruce told him. "My rules that keep us alive. And if you want to stay in this house, and on this team, then you'll abide by them!"

Dick's gaze broke first. "This is no partnership," he said flatly. "You're never going to trust me."

Bruce didn't say another word. He merely stood and watched Dick stride angrily away.

In his quarters in the mansion above, Alfred was finishing up recording a cassette tape. "I have tried every address I know for you," he was saying, referring to Wilfred. "I am praying this reaches you. We have very little time."

He slid the tape into an envelope as he heard a knock at the door and Bruce entered.

"Congratulations on your apprehension of Mr. Freeze, sir," Alfred said warmly. "It monopolized the evening news."

"Thanks," Bruce replied. But his voice was hollow; he seemed anything but celebratory.

"Is there something wrong, sir?" The old butler was immediately solicitous.

"Alfred . . ." Bruce said haltingly, then blurted out: "Am I pigheaded? Is it always 'my way or the highway'?"

"Why, yes, actually." Bruce's eyes widened at Alfred's reply. "Death and chance stole your parents. But rather than become a victim, you have done everything in your power to control the fates. For what is Batman if not an effort to master the chaos that sweeps our world — an attempt to control death itself?"

For an instant, Bruce's memory flashed back to a time when he was a boy. He remembered a windy night; he was standing by his parents' grave. There were tears frozen behind his young eyes as he struggled to come to terms with the murder of his beloved parents. His future would have been bleak and dark and empty . . . if Alfred hadn't been there. The old man had stood by him then, had stood by him ever since.

"But I can't control chaos, can I?" Bruce said softly, and Alfred shook his head.

"No. You can't. None of us can."

Down in the garage, a muted motorcycle engine died away. The headlight faded and went dark.

Stealthily, Barbara Wilson wheeled the competition racer back to its place in the line behind the cars and limos.

A hand reached out of the shadows to touch her shoulder, and Barbara reacted automatically. She grabbed the wrist, bent at the waist to take the weight on her hips, and whipped her assailant over her shoulder in an expert judo move. Ready to continue the attack, she spun — to face a floored Dick Grayson.

Barbara's demeanor changed immediately. "Oh, I'm so sorry," she said, with schoolgirl charm. "I'd just never seen anything like the bike. I took it out for a spin. I do hope it didn't inconvenience you."

Dick didn't reply, just raised a quizzical eyebrow as his gaze flicked over her tight leather costume.

"Ah yes, the outfit. For a costume party," Barbara lied. "Just trying it out. One never knows how leather will wear."

She reached out a hand and helped haul Dick to his feet. "Judo lessons at school, you know," she finished up. "I suppose they've taken better than I thought. Again, my greatest of pardons."

She hurried off before Dick had a chance to speak. He stared after her. Despite her explanation, he had a dozen questions he wanted answered. He turned with a shrug and made his way to the house.

Miles outside the city stood the nightmare gothic structure that was Arkham Asylum. Its charges had long since been given their medication, and the asylum's grim halls were relatively quiet.

Inside, several armed guards rolled a large subzero refrigerator on a gurney down a corridor. The fridge door was chained and padlocked shut. Mr. Freeze was jammed inside it, his face visible through the torn-off freezer compartment door.

"You're the common cold," the head guard sneered, "and we're the cure. Welcome home, Frost-Face!"

Freeze glared back. If he was troubled by his predicament, he didn't show it. "Allow me to break the ice. My name is Freeze. Learn it well — for it is the chilling sound of your doom."

A cell had been specially prepared. Glowing rings on the floor and ceiling projected a shimmering column of snowy cold within the center of the room.

Two guards hauled Freeze from his refrigerator. Even without his cryo-suit, the villain was an impressive sight. Muscles rippled on a taut body without a single ounce of fat. The guards were dragging him into the cold shield, when Freeze lashed out in sudden fury. A brutal fist took one guard in the head, while Freeze's foot came up sharply, to strike the other in the face.

Freeze rushed for the door. But as soon as his body passed out of the hypothermic shield, his knees buckled. Energy drained as he tumbled to his knees, his skin turning pallid gray. He began to wither and die.

"Look at him stew," one of the guards said, laughing and rubbing his bruised face. "How do you like your bad guy — medium, or well done?"

Every movement agony, every breath a laborious effort, Freeze turned and crawled back over the field threshold. At once, his color started to return to its normal white.

One of the guards stood at the wall sink, washing his hands. "Get used to it," he told Freeze. "You're gonna be here a very long time."

Freeze smiled, cold and deadly. "I'm afraid not. You see,

the means of my liberation is in your hands. Sadly, you will not live to see it."

In the run-down, crumbling heart of downtown Gotham, Poison Ivy and Bane made their way along a shadowed alley. Ahead of them lay the entrance to a long-abandoned Turkish bathhouse. Its doors were boarded up, but Bane's fists smashed through the heavy wood as if it were balsa.

"Batman and Birdbrain turned out to be more resistant to my charms than expected," Ivy said. "But no matter. I'll give them a stronger dose. Next time, they'll literally be dying for me."

The interior of the once-beautiful building stood in serious decay. The carved Middle Eastern furniture was crumbling away, mottled with damp. The formerly vivid murals that covered the walls were washed out and blurred, weeping color onto the tiled floor.

Ivy surveyed it, nodding with satisfaction. "A fixer-upper, yes. But with a certain homey charm."

Her eyes narrowed as a shadow seemed to detach itself from the wall. Then a second, and a third, till the entire chamber seemed to fill with sinister shapes.

"Ah, a minus," Ivy said, unworried. "Current tenants."

One figure stepped forward into the column of moonlight shining through a cracked window. His skin was pale and unhealthy, as if it had been years since he'd last seen sunlight.

"Hello, pretty," he breathed, eyes fixed on Ivy. This was Cannibal, leader of the Golum gang of urban predators. They slept by day and lived by night, and considered anything that came their way fair game.

"Hello yourself." Ivy's voice was light. "I love this place. I hope it's priced to sell."

"We love you." Cannibal's grin was a hideous parody, exposing his blackened teeth. "You look good enough to eat."

As Cannibal came menacingly toward her, Ivy moved. Her hand shot out and slammed the activation button on Bane's chest. Venom pumped from his backpack through the tubes fixed to the back of his skull. His muscles bulged and warped as if they had a life of their own.

The Golums threw themselves into the attack, but hitting Bane was like hitting a wall. He tossed them off like dolls, his huge fists beating a bloody tattoo on half a dozen faces. A Golum screamed as he was hurled through the air, crashing into a wall, and the survivors decided they'd had enough.

They turned and ran, leaving the wounded to make their own escape as best they could.

"For the strong, silent type, you are most persuasive," Ivy told Bane as he came to rest, almost like a robot. The criminal who had once been Antonio Diego was now addicted to the substance that warped his body so. As long as Ivy controlled his supply of Venom, he would have died for her.

Ivy walked across the floor. "Let's redecorate. First, the lighting is all wrong."

Bane reached up to grab a hanging board from the ceiling. He ripped it away, bringing a cascade of other boards crashing down. Sudden moonlight streamed in from outside.

"The floor?" Ivy asked.

The monster's foot stamped down hard, cracking the tiles, revealing the dirt beneath.

"Au naturel." Ivy nodded. "Still, I've always hankered for something on the water."

Bane's foot crashed down again, this time on an ancient water main. The thick pipe shattered and water gushed out, to be quickly absorbed by the thirsty soil. Ivy leaned over and took a bunch of tiny seeds from the satchel Bane carried. She dropped them to the ground, and waited.

Moments later, the mutant seeds sprouted. Tiny roots dug deep into the ground, as fast-growing vines emerged above. Fast-budding flowers popped open on the stems.

In her hand Ivy held the *Welcome to Gotham* bauble, and shook it so the snow swirled. "I've found a fellow who strikes my fancy," she said, more to herself than to the taciturn Bane. "A cool customer, yes. Icy demeanor, no question. But I detect a certain ruthless charm I may be able to use to my advantage."

She glanced at the lifeless bodies of the Golums on the floor. "Clean up the mess, Bane. We've got company coming."

In the sumptuous dining room at Wayne Manor, Alfred had set the table for two. The butler filled Bruce's goblet with mineral water, then turned away. His forehead beaded with sweat as he fought back the sudden pain that overwhelmed him.

Bruce didn't even notice. He was staring across the table at his dinner companion, Julie Madison.

But it wasn't Julie's face he was seeing. It was Poison Ivy's.

"Bruce, you're not even listening to me," Julie protested, and Bruce jerked out of his reverie. "We've been going out for a year now," Julie went on, "and . . ." She paused, taking a deep breath. "Okay, here goes. Bruce, I want to spend my life with you!"

Bruce shook his head, as much in surprise as to clear the vision of Poison Ivy that haunted him. "Julie, I'm not the marrying kind," he said gently. "There are things about me you wouldn't understand."

Bruce felt a twinge of guilt. Julie was a beautiful, intelligent girl — but he had used her more like a shield than a girlfriend. The media were always after Bruce Wayne; having Julie to focus on distracted them from ever connecting him with his Batman persona. He liked her. A lot. But that was as strong as his feelings ran. He certainly hadn't reckoned on Julie falling in love with him.

"You'll make a good husband," Julie was saying. "But I can't wait around forever, Bruce. Don't answer now. Just think it over."

She reached her face up toward him, her lips touching his. But even through closed eyes, it was the face of Poison Ivy that burned in Bruce's brain.

Fed up, his anger faded, Dick Grayson had returned to the Batcave. *Might as well use the time to see what good I can do,* he figured.

He'd called up a news photo of the survivors of the Flower Ball chaos, and it loomed large on his screen.

"Enhance detail, fourteen to nineteen," he rapped, and the computer obeyed instantaneously. A corner was highlighted, the image quickly expanding to fill the entire screen. Poison Ivy was unmistakable.

Dick gazed at it forlornly. "Who are you?" he said aloud, and his aching heart echoed the question.

The sudden whoop of an alarm jerked him back to reality. The screen image disappeared, overlaid by another: Barbara Wilson climbing out of her window, rappelling down the mansion wall.

"Gotcha!" Dick whistled, glad that he'd realigned the security monitors after seeing Barbara last night. The mystery was about to be solved!

In the garage, Barbara had donned her black leather and mounted the competiton bike. She kicked it into life, and peeled out into the night.

Seconds later, another bike followed, its headlight still off. Its rider didn't need lights; he knew this road like the back of his hand. Dick Grayson sped after his quarry.

CHAPTER

9

The crazy roaring of a hundred motorcycle engines echoed through the streets and split the Gotham night. The gangs were gathering for the races.

There were at least a dozen different biker gangs, from the all-black Midnites to the drug-dealing Street Demonz to the stone-killer Gotham Ghosts. Clad in leather, or denims, or rags. Hair swept back, or shaved off, or in dyed spikes. Tattoos and pierced faces. They'd have carved each other into oblivion long ago if someone hadn't come up with the idea of the bike races. Gang rider against gang rider, playing for cash and not for blood, side bets accepted. It had soon become a regular event.

Straddling the competition racer, Barbara weaved her way through the milling crowd and approached the Banker, the man in charge. "How much to play?" she asked.

"Two and a half."

Barbara pulled $250 out of her pocket, and handed it over. Another biker, the name *Spike* tattooed across his knuckles, stepped forward.

"You got a tag?"

"Call me Three-Jump," Barbara replied.

"You're the chick who won the run couple nights ago." It was a statement, not a question. "That was tricycle racing," Spike went on. "This is the real stuff. Maybe you wanna ride my hog instead?"

Barbara smiled slowly. "How about a side bet?"

As they moved into line next to the other racers, another figure emerged from the throng to pay his entry fee, his face obscured by his helmet. Barbara had no idea it was Dick Grayson.

A dozen engines revved and raged as the players strained impatiently for the signal. The Banker, his pockets swollen with three thousand dollars, raised a pistol in the air. He fired and the pack surged forward, shooting for prime position as they screamed toward the end of the alley.

They went shooting out into the street, a couple lofting up over the tops of cars, others using the stoops like a jump ramp. Barbara glanced sideways, to see the biker beside her go down in a pile of trash cans and garbage he hadn't noticed.

Two bikers shrieked neck and neck toward a racing truck. The truck driver's face froze in shock. But the bikers split at the last second, flying up off parked cars into the air. One spun out, sending its rider careening off, but the other came down at the head of the pack.

Racing down the straightaway toward the finish line, four bikes pulled away from the others. Among them were Barbara and Spike. One of the others hit an oil slick and veered out of control. The rider slid to safety, but the bike flew through the air. It smashed into a brick wall and turned into a fireball.

The finish was a series of flashing yellow warning beacons perched atop the incomplete construction of a drawbridge across the Gotham River. Barbara, Spike, and the incognito Dick Grayson raced toward it. The ground beneath their wheels changed from tar to riveted steel as they hit the bridge at full speed. Just beyond the line of flashing cones, an abyss separated the two raised, as yet unconnected, halves of the bridge.

The trick — which nobody had bothered to explain to either Dick or Barbara — was to cross the line first, but not so fast that you overshot and couldn't brake. Otherwise, you'd plunge into the dark water below.

Knowing what lay ahead, Spike hit his brakes before the other two. His mount slowed, falling out of position. Instead of slowing, both the other bikers gunned their engines even harder.

Barbara flashed past the line first, Dick's bike only a

hairsbreadth behind her. They both shot up over the edge of the unfinished bridge, soaring high above the watery abyss.

Dick's front wheel hit the metal roadway on the other side of the gap. It spun for a second, then gripped. Barbara wasn't so lucky. Her front wheel hit the edge badly. Dick looked over his shoulder, seeing her bike lose hold, slipping back over the edge.

Dick leaped from his still-moving bike, falling and rolling expertly on tucked shoulders. He ditched his helmet and vaulted toward the edge as Barbara's bike finally gave up the struggle. Bike and rider started to tumble down.

Dick's jump sent him over the edge after her, hands extended, feet catching the lip of the bridge in a precarious grip. His outstretched hand grasped Barbara's ankle. She jerked to a halt, her helmet falling off and plunging after the motorcycle into the waters below.

She looked up at her rescuer. Dick grinned back down at her. "So this is where you hang out at night," he quipped.

Five minutes later, they were back on the other side and Barbara was collecting her winnings from the Banker.

"I could have made it, you know," she told Dick crossly. "I didn't need your help."

Dick shrugged. "Whatever you say. It's all in a day's work for me."

Barbara held out her winnings. "This is toward replacing the bike I lost. I'll get you the rest."

"Keep it."

"Of course," Barbara said mockingly. "Dick Grayson, ward of the fabulously wealthy Bruce Wayne. Why would you need a few thousand dollars?"

Dick frowned. "Hey, what's your problem, Barbara?"

The girl shrugged, leather-clad shoulder reflecting a street light. "I guess the truth is, I'm just not comfortable with the idle rich. Even when they try to act like heroes."

Dick patted the pillion seat on his bike. "Better get comfortable real fast, sister. We only have one bike — and it's a long walk home!"

As they drove back to Wayne Manor, Barbara explained that she'd started racing after her parents died. There was something about the speed, the danger, that took her out of herself and made the hurt go away. She hadn't expected Dick to understand — but having lost his own parents so recently, so tragically, he knew exactly what she meant.

She revealed that she wasn't really on vacation, that she'd been expelled from the Academy in England for illicit bike racing. "But it doesn't matter," she concluded. "I've won enough money to do what I've always dreamed."

"Just don't tell me you're running away to join the circus," Dick said wryly.

By this time they were on the long drive that led up to the Manor. "Alfred has supported me my whole life," Barbara went on. "Now I'm going to pay him back. I'm going to liberate him from his dismal life of servitude!"

Dick's brow furrowed. "What are you talking about?"

They dismounted from the bike and wheeled it into the garage before Barbara replied. "Servants, masters — it's ridiculous! Alfred is the sweetest, most noble man alive, and he's subjugated all his life and dreams to someone else."

"Alfred and Bruce are like family," Dick protested.

They made their way up the steps to the house, and entered the foyer.

"Paying someone to prepare your meals and do your laundry and your dishes . . . you call that family?" Barbara demanded coldly.

"Alfred's happy here," Dick tried again.

"Happy?" Barbara said through clenched teeth. "You honestly don't know, do you? You can't even see what's in front of your own eyes."

They'd reached the main stairs, shrouded in darkness. Dick paused and turned to look at her, puzzled.

"Look at his skin," Barbara said. "At how he's hiding the pain all the time. Can't you see it? Alfred's sick!"

Without waiting for his reply, she ran up the stairs to her room.

"Alfred's not sick."

Dick started as he heard Bruce's voice. Bruce was wreathed in shadows, sitting at the side of the stairs. "He's dying."

Dick could scarcely believe it. "But . . . he never said a word —"

"You know Alfred. He'd never say anything. But I've had my suspicions. I've been watching him. He saved my life, Dick." The older man hesitated, before going on, almost awkwardly. "And I've never told him how I feel."

"Talk to him, Bruce," Dick urged. Their squabble earlier was completely forgotten in their shared anxiety for the old man. "There's nothing worse than losing someone without telling them how you feel."

Bruce looked away, staring into darkness. Memories of his parents rose unbidden in his mind. "I know," he said softly. "I know."

CHAPTER

10

Mr. Freeze huddled in the anti-thermic field in the center of his Arkham cell. With painstaking care, he was crafting a tiny ice sculpture of his beloved wife. Completing it, he lifted the miniature gearworks from an alarm clock and placed the ice sculpture on top of it.

The delicate statuette began to turn, like a figure in a music box.

Freeze looked up at the sound of a guard's voice. "Hey, Icehead. You got a visitor. Your sister."

Freeze frowned. Sister? He had no sister.

The guard unlocked the cell, and a second guard ushered in a woman enveloped in a large cloak.

The asylum's basement housed a room with a single barred window, where inmates' belongings were kept until their owners were deemed fit enough for release. Mannequins displayed several famous costumes, representing the villains who were presently incarcerated, including the Riddler's green one-piece covered in question marks, as well as Mr. Freeze's silver cryonic costume.

An elderly guard sat with his chair against the wall, watching television. Suddenly, two fists smashed through the cement wall behind him and grabbed the sides of the chair. His mouth fell open in surprise. He didn't even have time to yell before the chair — and him with it — was wrenched back through the wall in a storm of dust and debris.

Seconds later, Bane entered via the same hole in the wall, and made straight for Freeze's cryo-suit.

"Don't mind us, ma'am," one guard said, upstairs. "You can converse freely with your brother."

"Oh, I don't mind you at all." Poison Ivy shrugged off the voluminous cloak she was wrapped in, revealing her skintight green costume. The two guards stood as if mesmerized, overwhelmed by the aura she radiated.

"What if I told you one kiss from me could kill you?"

The guards sighed, unable to care about anything except this ravishing woman whose finger on their cheeks felt like love fire. Gently, Ivy touched each with her lips.

"I really am to die for," she said cruelly. She watched ca-

sually as the guards grasped at their throats and fell chok-
ing to the floor.

She heard an alarm sound in the distance. *No doubt
somebody spotted Bane,* she thought. No matter. Her
Venom-pumped slave could take everything they might
throw at him and still walk away the winner.

"Impressive." Mr. Freeze had been watching everything.

"My most unabominable snowman," Ivy returned, "I
have also been impressed with you. I propose a pairing. So
I'm here to set you free."

"An enticing offer. But what does the lady want in return?"

"Let's cool it for now," Ivy stalled. "There's someone I
want you to meet."

She pressed a button on the cell console, and the door
slid noiselessly open. Bane entered, wheeling Freeze's
cryo-suit on a gurney. Ivy couldn't help noting the blood
on the gurney wheels; someone had got in his way, and
paid for it.

She sealed the door behind him.

"His name is Bane," Ivy introduced him to Freeze. Bane
rolled the cart across the cryonic field. Freeze grabbed his
costume and started to put it on.

"A laundry service that delivers," he joked. "Thank you,
Mr. Bane."

With his costume and helmet snapped back into place,

Ivy couldn't help thinking, Freeze was an even more impressive figure. But the villain was glancing at his watchlike status display. His power supply was exhausted, running on auxiliary only. The fuel compartments in his sleeves, which should have held the all-important diamonds, were depleted.

"I'm running on empty," he told Ivy. "I need the diamonds from my hideout."

Ivy posed coquettishly. "I can help you get them," she breathed.

"Batman and Robin may be waiting," Freeze warned. "In my weakened state I'm no match for them."

"You leave those boys to me," Ivy said firmly.

The flame of a laser torch cut suddenly through the steel door, and began to slice an entry. The guards!

"Bane, an exit, if you please." Poison Ivy thumped the Venom pump, and Bane groaned as the power of the awful drug shot through him. His massive fists slammed against the far wall, but to no avail. Plaster cracked and split, but the steel-reinforced concrete beneath didn't break.

Freeze walked to the sink, and swiftly turned on the water. This was what he'd referred to earlier, when he taunted the guard.

The hole in the cell door was growing larger, and they could hear the shouts of the guards in the hall beyond. Holding his gauntlet underneath the running water, Freeze cracked the seal. Cryo-gas hissed out.

"Always winterize your pipes," the villain said, laughing, as he aimed the gas jet at the spigot. Instantly pipes around the room began to freeze, expanding as the water in them turned to ice. They bulged briefly before cracking open, buckling and warping wildly. A frozen shock wave ran before them, splitting the wall in a dozen places.

Ivy peered out from the turreted cell into the moonlit night. Far below, she could hear the rushing waters of the river.

"While I get my diamonds," Freeze said, "you and Meatloaf will retrieve my wife. We'll rendezvous in your lair, if you trust me to know where it is."

"Hold it," Ivy hissed. She perched precariously on the jagged wall. "You never said anything about a wife!"

"You want to be partners?" Freeze asked. "Then bring me my snowy bride."

Just then the cell door flew off its hinges and guards rushed in. Without a backward glance, the three villains launched themselves through the shattered wall into the night air.

They dropped together, the swirling waters rushing up to meet them.

"So where do I find Mrs. Frigidaire?" Ivy asked, moments before the Gotham River closed over their heads.

Alfred was doing his rounds, flicking out the lights as he put Wayne Manor to bed for the night. Beside him, Bruce Wayne walked slowly.

"Alfred, I know you're sick," the younger man began. "I can get you the best doctors . . ."

"I've seen the best doctors," Alfred said testily, then drew himself up and recovered his composure. "A gentleman does not discuss his ailments, sir. It's not civilized."

Bruce bit back a bitter smile. He'd known his butler a long time. There was no point pressing him when he was like this. Abruptly, Bruce changed the subject. "Have you ever regretted your life working here, Alfred?"

The old man shook his head. "Attending to heroes? No, sir," he said adamantly. "My only regret is that I was never able to be out there with you."

"Not all heroes wear masks," Bruce said softly, and Alfred smiled. "Alfred, if I've never told you . . . I just wanted to say . . ."

Alfred looked at him, expectant. He knew how difficult it was for his master to express his emotions. "Yes, sir?"

They turned at the sound of running steps, and the moment passed. Dick was hurrying toward them, his voice urgent. "Freeze has escaped!"

CHAPTER

11

An hour later, a dozen police cruisers had converged on the Snowy Cones Ice Cream Factory. The Batmobile was also there, parked out of sight in a shadowed alleyway.

While Gotham PD forensic units went over every square inch of the factory in search of clues, Batman and Robin examined the interior of the ice villain's lair. So far, at least, there appeared to be no indication as to what Freeze intended to do next.

Police Commissioner James Gordon produced a portable monitor; the videotape running on it showed the villains' daring aerial escape. "We pulled these off the surveillance cameras at Arkham," the police chief said. "But what makes you think Freeze will come back here?"

Batman gestured around the lab. "His freezing engine, his weapons, his gems. They're the keys to his power." He studied the film for a moment, lips pursed, then Gordon thrust forward a photograph.

"From the security camera at Gotham Airport," the policeman said. "A few nights ago."

The shot was grainy and slightly blurred; it showed a cloaked woman walking alongside a giant form, also in disguise. "These two arrived on a charter from South America," Gordon explained. "They put ten security guards in the hospital, left a businessman dead of organic poisoning, and stole his limousine."

"The same pair that sprang Freeze," Batman said grimly. "But why would Poison Ivy help Freeze escape?"

"She's evil," Robin said emphatically, as if that explained all.

Robin waited while Gordon headed off, then went on quietly: "It's weird — for a while, Ivy was all I could think about. It was almost like I . . . loved her. But then . . ."

Batman nodded as his partner's voice trailed off. "I know. The feeling just vanished."

"I can't believe we were fighting over a bad guy."

"Bad, yes," Batman nodded. "But guy? No. This is one majorly beautiful evil woman."

"I'm totally over her," Robin said confidently. "Positively."

"Me too," Batman agreed.

But even as they spoke, the faint, lingering image of Poison Ivy flitted through both their minds.

Batman walked over to the large walk-in freezer and examined the wall of food there. He thought for a second, then his hand closed around a frozen Chinese dinner. "'Open Sesame Chicken,'" he read off the box. Just the sort of thing that would appeal to Freeze's sense of humor.

Batman lifted the box — and the entry to the secret vault swung open.

The two heroes entered, and saw the frosty sarcophagus before them. They realized at once that here was the solution to the mystery of Nora Fries.

"She's still alive," Batman muttered. "He's adapted his freezing technology to reverse McGregor's Syndrome." Quickly, he flicked through the notebooks that were stacked there — the records of Freeze's every experiment. "He's even found a cure for the early stages of the disease."

Behind a slatted floor vent, a pair of eyes screwed in concentration as they watched Batman and Robin examine the container and its frozen human contents. Poison Ivy thanked her lucky stars she'd taken Freeze's advice and entered via the ventilation system.

"Can Freeze save her?" Robin asked, and Batman shook his head.

"No. Her case is too advanced. But maybe someday, with more research —"

He broke off, puzzled, as several spirals of glittering fairy dust wafted from a wall vent. Dazed, almost zombielike, Batman and Robin bent to rip off the grate. Beyond it stretched a vast industrial basement that contained dozens of huge ice cream vats. Bane stood close to the grille, at the top of a flight of steps.

"No beauty," Batman said.

"Just the beast," Robin added.

They were already rushing the monster, whose chest and biceps bulged with the Venom he'd absorbed. Almost casually, Bane sideswiped Robin, a heavy blow that sent him thudding to the floor. Then Bane and Batman faced each other for the first time.

Batman moved into the attack first, unleashing a fluid combination of blows that would have felled any ordinary man. But, buoyed by the powerful drug, Bane hardly seemed to notice Batman's attack. His own fists lashed out in brutal rhythm, and Batman had no choice but to fall back. A punch caught him, stunning him momentarily; but it was long enough for the brute. Bane followed through, hard, and Batman fell to the floor.

As Robin picked himself up, Ivy showed herself, moving out from behind the vats. Before Robin could react, she'd blown a handful of her Love Dust right in his face.

"Polly want a kiss?" Ivy leaned close, smiling at him, and her beauty made his heart ache. But he had to fight against her power. Batman needed help!

"I must be losing my touch," Ivy pouted, as Robin ignored her and rushed to his partner's aid.

Upstairs, the policemen combing the abandoned factory looked up in surprise as the heavy front doors suddenly blew open. Mr. Freeze was framed there, looking harassed and weak from the heat.

"I hate uninvited guests," he snarled, reaching to pull a lever marked COOLANT GAS. At once, blue freezing gas began to hiss from every grille and vent. Policemen started to cough and choke, shivering uncontrollably as the intense cold gnawed at them.

Robin could never hope to take down Bane in a face-to-face confrontation, but the hero did have speed and agility on his side. He was able to dart in and out, striking the monster and retreating again before being hit himself. Anything to distract Bane from doling out more punishment to Batman, who'd rolled clear — straight into Poison Ivy.

A glittering cloud of dust blew into his face, and he shook his head to try and clear it. "Why do all the gorgeous villains have to be homicidal maniacs?" he complained. "Is it me?"

"You bring out the animal in me," Ivy purred.

"Then I should have brought my leash!" Batman shot back.

Another cloud of dust wafted from Ivy's palm to envelop Batman. The villainess pouted, licking her lips, leaning closer as if to kiss the Dark Knight. But at the last moment, Batman used every ounce of his willpower to avert his face.

"You're going to jail," he hissed.

"I'm a lover, not a fighter," Ivy rejoined. "That's why every Poison Ivy action figure comes complete with . . . him."

She gestured, and Batman turned — to find Bane standing directly behind him. In the background, Robin lay on the floor, winded and groaning. Batman felt himself seized in a grip of steel, and hoisted bodily over Bane's head.

Then he was hurtling through the air, to crash into a wall with painful impact.

"I'm off to kiss bachelor number two." Ivy turned away. "Try not to make a mess when you die."

Bane advanced on the fallen Batman, fists clenching and unclenching, as if he couldn't wait to murder Gotham's premier hero. But Batman feinted, then coiled and leaped. The impact sent Bane sprawling.

Mr. Freeze stuffed a handful of fuel gems from his secret safe into his suit compartments. A wave of bitter cold swept through him as the costume powered up, and he sighed with relief.

"Chilled to perfection," he breathed, heading off toward his storage lockers, leaving a half-dozen frozen policemen in his wake.

Commissioner Gordon shivered, barely able to force his frozen limbs into action. He reached for the switch marked EMERGENCY HEAT with a trembling hand, and forced it down. Hidden circuits sprang into life, sending a warming glow through the whole room. Dripping, skin blue, the policemen thawed back to life.

"Stop living in the shadow of the big bad Bat!" Poison Ivy hissed. She had pressed Robin up against an ice cream vat, her face close to his. "You deserve your own legend. How about your own bright, shining signal in the sky? Let me guide you. Let me" — she leaned even closer — "kiss you."

As if hypnotized, Robin felt powerless to resist. His eyelids fluttered behind his mask, and despite himself he moved toward her. But before their lips could meet, a tiny Batarang zipped through the air and stung his cheek.

Batman stood there. "Remember the victim at the airport," he chided. "Toxins introduced through the mouth."

Robin frowned. "What are you talking about?"

Batman indicated Ivy, who took several steps back from Robin. "Why is she so desperate to kiss us? I'm betting that her lips are poison."

"A poison kiss?" Robin snorted with derision. "You have some real issues with women, you know that?" He turned toward Batman, his voice rising, his eyes grim and threatening. "You just couldn't stand that she was about to kiss *me!*" He shoved Batman in the chest. "You couldn't stand that something might be *mine* and not yours. Could you?"

Robin shoved him again, harder this time. Batman could

see his partner was in no condition to reason. Whatever Ivy was doing to them, Robin had swallowed it hook, line, and sinker. Reluctantly, Batman's fist shot out, sending Robin flying backward — into a vat filled with frost and snow.

But if Batman had hoped it would cool his partner down, he was wrong. "Ivy's right," Robin said hotly, shrugging off Batman's attempt to help him out of the vat. "I don't need you. I'm going solo!"

"What happened?" Commissioner Gordon's voice cut into their squabble. "How did they get away?"

Feeling slightly foolish, Batman looked around the room. Ivy and Bane were gone.

The hidden chamber where Nora Fries slept her eternal sleep was deserted now. A floor vent opened, and Poison Ivy rose quickly through it.

She stared at the frozen woman in the capsule before her. "I'm just not good with competition," she admitted, and reached for the plug connecting the power supply. She yanked it hard, and turned to leave the way she'd entered.

She felt no compunction about the fact that she'd just murdered another human being. What had happened to Pamela Isley in that South American jungle had hardened her heart against all humans. Every single one of them could perish, and her only emotion would be joy.

CHAPTER

12

Poison Ivy's plant magic had transformed the Blossom Street Turkish Baths. Dawn broke, and sunlight streamed in, illuminating the host of plants within. Vines and shrubs vied with flowers of all shapes and colors, in a riot of luxuriant vegetation.

Ivy entered the small anteroom where Mr. Freeze sat with the Freezing Engine he'd managed to take from his hideout. He was zapping the walls with its frozen beam, turning the room into a miniature world of ice.

"Make yourself right at home."

Freeze glared at the sound of Ivy's voice. "Where is my wife?"

Ivy looked suddenly upset. "There . . . there was nothing I could do," she said sincerely. "Batman deactivated her. She's dead."

"You lie!" The words burst from Freeze like an explosion. He lunged at Ivy, but Bane stepped quickly between them. Bolstered by his cryo-suit's power, Freeze hurled the Venom addict across the room. Bane rolled to his feet, ready to fight, but Ivy stilled him with a gesture.

"I'm sorry," Ivy whispered. She held something up in her hand, and Freeze winced with pain as he saw it. Nora's snowflake necklace.

He reached to take it. When he spoke, his voice was cold with hatred. "Their bones will turn to ice. Their blood will freeze in my hands."

"Kill them? Of course." Ivy hesitated a moment. Freeze was in an emotional state, perfect for her to goad into following her own scheme. "But why stop there?" she went on. "Why should only Batman and Robin die while the society that created them goes unpunished?"

She lifted the frozen Gotham bauble off the iced table, and absentmindedly turned it over in her hand. Freeze stared at her, well aware that she was trying to manipulate him for her own ends. But he'd planned to ice the city anyway; only now, there would be no ransom demand.

"Yes," he agreed. "I shall repay the world for sentencing me to a life without the warmth of human comfort. I will blanket Gotham City in endless winter. First Gotham — then the world!"

Ivy smiled, satisfied. "Just what I had in mind. Everything dead on Earth except us. A chance for Mother Nature to start again." She lifted a flower, contemplating its fragile petals. "Plants and flowers are the oldest species on the planet, yet they are defenseless against man." She spoke directly to the flower: "Sorry, honey, but this is for science." She crushed it in her hand and announced dramatically, "Behold the dawn of a new age!"

At Ivy's command, Bane rolled in a canister with PROJECT GILGAMESH stencilled on its side. Bane stood well back as Ivy opened it and pulled out a strange, otherworldly plant. Its head moved around, as if it could see, the stalks at its center like hissing fangs.

"I have created a race of plants with the powers of the deadliest animals," Ivy told Freeze. Despite his grief at his wife's death, the villain looked impressed. "Once you have frozen humankind," she went on, "my mutants will overrun the globe. The Earth will become a brave new world of only plants. And we shall rule them — for we will be the only two people left!"

"Adam and Evil." Freeze picked up the Gotham bauble, and held it on his palm. His gauntlet glowed blue, and the tiny city was instantly frozen. Freeze's hand closed, inexorably crushing the toy to shards of ice. "You will distract the Bat and Bird while I prepare to freeze Gotham," he told Ivy.

"Can't we just ice them along with the rest of the citizenry?"

Freeze scowled. "That is far too merciful. Batman will watch his beloved Gotham perish. Then *I* will kill him!"

"As a team," Ivy said thoughtfully, "the Duncely Duo protect each other. But Robin is young. Impetuous. If I could get him alone..." She smiled as an idea struck her. "The way to a boy's heart is through his ego. What strapping young hero could resist his very own signal?"

"It's Stage One of McGregor's Syndrome," Dr. Lyle announced. "I'm sorry. All we can do is make him comfortable."

It was night now. The doctor stood in the hallway outside Alfred's room at Wayne Manor. Beside him, Dick and Barbara looked grim and serious. Through the part-open door they could see into the dim room. Alfred lay in bed, pale and weak. Bruce sat beside him, bent in grief.

"I've spent my whole life trying to beat back death," Bruce was saying. "Everything I've done — everything I'm capable of — but I can't save you."

Alfred's voice was faint, but calm and unhurried. "Everybody dies, Master Bruce. There's no defeat in that. Victory comes in defending what we know is right while we still live."

Tentatively, Bruce reached out to take the old man's hand in his. "I love you," he said softly.

Alfred's face was wan, but his eyes blazed clear and

bright. "Remember this always. I'm proud of you, son. And I love you, too."

When the doctor left, Dick followed Bruce downstairs. The billionaire was dressed in a tuxedo, and now he pulled on his overcoat. He and Julie had a date at the opening of the observatory.

"McGregor's Syndrome," Dick said. "That's what Freeze's wife had."

"Yes. But Alfred's condition is less severe. Freeze's research notes say he cured a case like Alfred's. They just don't say how."

Dick sighed. "I checked the medical database. No one else is even close."

Bruce headed for the front door. "I'm late for the dedication. Then I go after Freeze and Ivy. Alone."

"You do not!" Dick spat the words out. Since his second dose of Ivy's dust, he'd become even more infatuated with her.

"Dick, don't push me right now," Bruce said evenly.

"Or what?" the younger man challenged. "No one can capture Ivy but the big, bad Bat? Nonsense! You just want her for yourself, don't you? Admit it!"

"Yes!" Bruce answered frankly. "Yes, I want her so badly I can taste it. And that's the whole point. We're perfect targets. She's done something to us, somehow got us fighting over her again!"

"Hail the all-knowing Bruce Wayne," Dick sneered. "Here's what *I* know: Ivy loves me. Me, not you. And it's driving you crazy. It's why you stopped us from kissing. Because if you can't have her, nobody can!"

"She's clouded your mind," Bruce accused. "You're not thinking straight!"

"Oh, but I am," Dick returned. "For the first time in a long time. I'm through living in your shadow. All that ends right now!"

Bruce bit back his angry words as the boy stalked off. Dick had always been volatile — but whatever Ivy had done to them had made him ten times worse. A thought alien to his very nature popped into Bruce's mind: *What if the villains win?*

Barbara had taken over Bruce's vigil by Alfred's bedside, her heart breaking. "I'm sorry," she said softly. "I was too late. I only wanted to take you away from this place, give you a chance to live your own life. You don't deserve to be a slave."

"A slave? Oh no, child!" Alfred protested weakly. "I have been part of the greatest adventure ever known. I have found purpose here, and the family I could never have."

He smiled, then braced himself as pain stabbed through him. "You must do something for me, Barbara." He slid an envelope out from under his pillow, and put it in her hand. "Find my brother Wilfred. Give him this. I have duties he must fulfill in my stead. Only family can be trusted."

Barbara weighed the envelope in her hand. "What is it?"

"It is the sacred trust of two good men whom I have had the honor of calling 'son.' Take it — but I implore you, never open it." Alfred reached up to touch Barbara's cheek. "You look so like your mother," he said tenderly, his voice trailing away.

His eyes closed, and he fell into a troubled sleep.

CHAPTER

13

The official unveiling of the telescope at the restored Gotham Observatory attracted every socialite in the city. Prominent among them, of course, was the man whose money had paid for it all, Bruce Wayne. Julie Madison was pretty as a picture, linked to his arm, laughing and cracking jokes with the ever-present media mob.

Pamela Isley stood alone in the center of the room, her drab outfit and demeanor making her anything but a conversation magnet. She saw Commissioner Gordon making his way through the throng, greeting friends and acquaintances.

"I've always wondered," Pamela said, as Gordon reached for a drink from a waiter's tray, "where does that big old Bat-light come from?"

The Commissioner turned to her, glass in hand. Pamela flipped open a compact, as if she was about to powder her face. But she blew into it, and the fine, glittering dust that rested there wafted over the police chief. Gordon breathed deep. It was as if he'd been kicked in the heart by a mule. He'd never seen anyone so beautiful as this wonderful girl.

A faint trace of the dust blew on past Gordon, shimmering slightly in the air around Bruce Wayne.

"The Bat-Signal?" the Commissioner repeated to Pamela. The dust had sapped his will, until all he wanted was to please this woman. "Why, it's on top of police headquarters."

Pamela took the Commissioner's arm and led him like a lovesick puppy into an alcove. "I'd just love to see it," she gushed. "But I don't suppose you have access."

Gordon puffed out his chest. "Why, I'm Commissioner of Police!" He patted his pocket. "I have the keys right here."

Bruce and Julie were surrounded by a gaggle of reporters and well-wishers. But it was Julie who was doing all the talking, as Bruce looked around him distractedly. He felt strange, almost longing for . . . what? He didn't know. He caught a glimpse of Gordon in the alcove, and mumbling some apology, Bruce peeled away toward him.

Gordon had his back to the alcove wall. He felt wonderful. He couldn't believe that such a gorgeous girl was spending time with an old fogy like him. Pamela pressed close to him. Her hand slid inside his jacket pocket.

Gordon was stunned when she suddenly announced: "On second thought, you're way too old for me."

She pushed him aside and walked briskly to the door, tossing something in her hand. Gordon's keys.

As she was about to exit, a hand grasped her arm. "Dr. Isley." It was Bruce. He stared at her, rapt. "You're . . . enchanting. The most beautiful woman I've ever seen. If you're, um, free this evening . . ."

Pamela frowned, unaware that Bruce, too, had been exposed to her Love Dust.

Julie Madison's pretty face was darkened by a thunderous frown as she came up to join them. "Bruce?" she asked her boyfriend. "What are you doing?"

Pamela smiled smugly. "He's asking me on a date, in an awkward, stammering sort of way," she crowed.

Julie was incredulous. "You're asking another woman out — right in front of me?"

Several people had overheard the exchange, and conversation around them muted as people craned to hear more. Sensing a story, reporters had their pens poised to record every word.

"I am?" Bruce said. Then he repeated it, as if it was no longer a question: "I am."

Julie glared, absolutely furious. "Make a choice, Bruce," she said through thin lips. "Her or me."

"Well, um . . ." Bruce knew he shouldn't be doing this, drawing attention, making fools of himself and Julie. But somehow he couldn't seem to help it. He hadn't even noticed the Love Dust he'd inhaled. "Her," he said finally, embarrassed, looking to Pamela.

"You've made your point," Julie said sadly. She was crestfallen, as if all the spirit had drained out of her. "You really aren't the marrying kind. Good-bye, Bruce Wayne!"

Fighting back tears of anger and hurt, she pushed through the throng and was gone.

Bruce felt like a heel as he turned to smile at Pamela. She gestured after the departing Julie. "Physical perfection, charm, and wealth . . . rejected in favor of a dowdy spinster. How do you explain your behavior, Mr. Wayne?"

Bruce shook his head, puzzled. "I can't. But perhaps tonight, over dinner . . . "

Pamela didn't let him finish. "Maybe your witless playboy persona works on all the bimbos — but I am not the least bit interested in your attention. So back off" — she jabbed a finger in the surprised Bruce's chest — "or I'll have you in court quicker than you can spell 'sexual harassment'!"

People stared, murmuring to each other. Bruce felt helpless as Pamela pushed past him.

"Does that mean dinner's a no?" he asked foolishly. But Pamela Isley had obtained what she'd come for. She was already gone.

Mr. Freeze had turned the anteroom at the Blossom Street baths into his own personal ice chamber. He breathed deeply in the frigid air as he snapped his costume into place. A new legion of Icemen had been hired; they waited in the swirling, freezing mist.

"Bundle up, boys," Freeze told them. "There's a storm coming."

Carrying his ingenious Freezing Engine, he and his battalion headed out into the night.

On the roof of Gotham police headquarters, a heavy door swung open. Bane and Poison Ivy exited onto the flat roof.

"Let there be light," Ivy said, giggling, as Bane strained his muscles and ripped the heavy Bat-Signal from its shackles.

"Only family can be trusted?"

Barbara Wilson repeated her uncle Alfred's words. She was in her room at the Manor, the envelope he'd given her still clutched in her hand. Well, she was family, wasn't she?

She slit the envelope open and withdrew a single silver compact disc. Hesitating only for a moment, she slid it into the slot in her computer's hard drive.

ACCESS DENIED, PROTECTED FILES, she read on the screen.

"Perhaps you didn't give me your genes, Uncle Alfred," Barbara said to herself, "but you gave me your heart."

Patiently, methodically, she set about hacking into the disc.

Nobody at the observatory gala had been surprised when Bruce made his excuses and left for home. Still dressed in his tuxedo, he hurried up to see Alfred. The old butler was asleep. He was hooked up to life support now, his strength weakening with every passing hour.

Bruce sighed deeply, then made his way down into the hall. Stepping behind the grandfather clock, he stood in the secret tunnel that led down to the Batcave.

Minutes later, he sat glumly at the main computer console, distraught. Memories of Alfred ran through his head — the good times they'd had together, the way the butler had been there right from the start of his life as the Batman. Why, they'd even designed the costume together.

"Criminals are a superstitious, cowardly lot," a younger Alfred had impressed on him. "Your costume must strike fear into their hearts."

Bruce groaned aloud. "Old friend, I could use your help right now."

"Right here, sir," a brisk English voice announced.

Bruce spun around, amazed at what he saw. A monitor had flickered into life, the words COMPUTER SIMULATION flashing under an image of Alfred.

"I anticipated a moment might arrive when I became incapacitated," the screen image was saying. "Therefore I programmed my brain algorithms into the Batcomputer and created a simulation."

Bruce stared for a long moment before his face relaxed into a smile. "It's good to see you."

"What seems to be the problem, sir?"

"You are," Bruce replied softly.

The image seemed to stare back at him. "Surely, I am not the only cause of your distress."

It was true — there was something else. "Women," Bruce said curtly. "First, Ivy had an intoxicating effect on both Dick and me. Tonight my feelings spread to someone else, Pamela Isley. I was so attracted to her, I couldn't reason clearly. I still can't." He became brisker, more focused. "She used to work for Wayne Enterprises. Find a file, Alfred."

"Coming on-line now, sir," the virtual butler replied. He'd scarcely finished before the screen filled with photos, reports, and files. "Dr. Isley was researching advanced botany. DNA splicing. Recombinant animal-plant patterns. Pheromone extraction."

"Pheromones?" Bruce echoed.

"Glandular secretions from animals, sir," Alfred explained. "Scents that create powerful emotions, like fear and rage."

"And passion!" Bruce finished for him. "Of course!" It

was as if a lightbulb had gone on in his head. "Find the photo of Poison Ivy after the Flower Ball."

The image dutifully appeared beside the one of Pamela Isley. "Deconstruct and resolve," Bruce ordered, already knowing what the experiment would achieve.

Schematics of various features — fingerprints, retina scans, height, and weight — were all highlighted and compared. All matched perfectly. Pamela Isley and Poison Ivy were one and the same person.

Suddenly, an alert started to flash, and an alarm sounded. Alfred's simulated voice was dry as he said, "It appears, sir, that someone has stolen the Bat-Signal."

In her room, Barbara was still trying to find the access code that would unlock the secrets of the silver disc. She typed in yet another attempted password: MARGARET.

ACCESS DENIED, the screen flashed.

Barbara glared in frustration. Then a sudden idea came. Fingers flying, she typed PEG on the keyboard.

ACCESS CODE ACCEPTED.

Barbara nodded with satisfaction. She hit a key and sat back, shocked and amazed at the images that scrolled before her eyes.

CHAPTER

14

Since his immersion in the cryogenic solution had driven him nearly insane, Mr. Freeze had made millions of dollars from his criminal activities. Much of that money had been spent on research into his wife's condition, and most of the remainder had gone into equipping himself and his various gangs of thugs. He paid them well, on retainer, knowing that he could summon them whenever they were required.

Such as now.

Freeze's trucks screeched to a halt on a Gotham side street. Freeze and Bane were in the lead cab. They looked up into the night sky where, high above them, overhanging the city from its tall cliff, the Gotham Observatory stood. The giant viewing slit in the dome was open, the telescope aimed up at the stars.

"It's going to be a long, cold night," Freeze muttered darkly.

Closer to the center of the city, other equipment was pointed at the night sky. The Bat-Signal blazed, projected on a low cloud, the time-honored message that the city needed its protector.

Then something amazing happened. The familiar beacon began to change, its color draining away, then turning bright red. The shape within changed from a stylized bat to a stylized bird.

A Robin-Signal beamed over the city.

In the Batcave, the monitor pulsed with the new signal. Bruce Wayne watched as Dick threw on his crimefighter costume.

"That's no Bat-light," Robin said proudly. He knew Poison Ivy had been at work. "It's a birdcall!"

"Her real name is Pamela Isley," Bruce informed him. "I saw her talking to Gordon at the gala. She must have stolen his keys, altered the signal."

"And she did it all for me," Dick said, in a tone of admiration. "For love."

Bruce tried to cut through his young ward's cocky optimism. "She's infected us with some kind of chemical extract, Dick!"

"Oh yeah?" Dick scoffed. "Is that it? I'm under some kind of magic spell?"

Bruce's voice was flat as he strove to remain calm. "She wants to kill you."

"You'd say anything to keep me away from her," Dick accused. The pheromones of Ivy's Love Dust still coursed through his bloodstream, ensuring that he stayed besotted with her. "To keep her for yourself!"

Bruce shook his head. "You once said to me that being part of a team means trusting your partner. That sometimes counting on someone else is the only way to win. Do you remember?"

Dick turned his head away, not answering.

"You weren't just talking about partners," Bruce went on. "You were talking about being a family. Well, one of our family is dying. I don't want to lose everyone I've ever cared about." He paused, staring hard at Dick until the boy literally had to return his gaze. "I'm asking you now, friend . . . partner . . . brother. Will you trust me?"

On the tower platform at the observatory, a scientist and his aide stood amid the leftovers from the gala party, testing the telescope. It was precision weighted, balanced on a huge tracking arm that jutted out of the observatory dome and overhung the cliff.

There was a tremendous crashing noise from below, and seconds later Bane and Mr. Freeze entered.

"Sorry about the door," Freeze greeted them. "Is the party over?"

The scientists stared as Bane pulled several explosive charges from his satchel and started setting them around the room near the telescope's base.

"Who is that nutball?" a scientist demanded.

Freeze scowled and pointed his weapon upward. A cryonic blast engulfed the hapless man. "That's Mr. Nutball to you," the villain sneered. "Hmm . . . half a set of bookends." He contemplated the frozen scientist, and turned to his aide. "You — copy him." The terrified aide followed suit, mimicking his frozen boss's pose.

A second blast of cryonic energy struck the aide, freezing him solid. Freeze laughed. "A matched pair. Sometimes I exceed even my wildest expectations." He glanced up at the barrel of the mighty telescope. "If revenge is a dish best served cold, then put on your Sunday finest," he said menacingly. "It's time to feast!"

The Batcave lay dark and dormant, until the automatic activation sequence engaged. Ambient lights glowed into life. Computers flickered. The giant Batmobile pedestal began to rise. On it stood no car, but a single figure. Barbara.

Overwhelmed by the cave's grandeur, and the high-tech equipment that packed so many parts of it, she walked across to the main console. After a moment's thought, she hit a button. The Alfred simulation popped up on the screen.

"Uncle Alfred?" Barbara was amazed.

"In spirit only," the image replied.

"The boys need help."

There was a pause, as the image of the old man seemed to stare at her. Then: "Your mother would be proud," it said.

The main screen filled with schematics of costumes. Barbara smiled as the image of her uncle asked, "Forgive my being personal, dear girl — but I must know your measurements."

Robin had tracked the mysterious Bird-Signal to its source: the abandoned Turkish baths on Blossom Street. He passed the heavy metal signal chained to the door, and looked around in surprise at the lush plant growth that seemed to burst from every nook and cranny.

The light shut off as he went inside.

The interior was something no human could ever have imagined. Large floral fans rotated lazily, circulating the warm air. Curtains of multicolored leaves undulated in the slight breeze. Fruit burst with color. In the center of the room was a bedlike platform made out of flower buds. Poison Ivy reached to stroke them gently, and they instantly blossomed.

She heard a slight noise, and looked up as Robin entered.

Ivy smiled, and extended her hand toward him.

On the observatory tower platform, Mr. Freeze finished hooking up his Freezing Engine to the telescope itself. Bane finished laying his explosive charges, and came silently over to join him.

"Big family?" Freeze asked. "Like pets? Don't talk much, do you?"

Freeze knew there was no point waiting for Bane to reply. He wouldn't. Freeze engaged the engine, and the entire pedestal was washed in a blue wave of freezing cryonic energy.

The ambient ice wave spread down from the telescope, encasing the building below. Outside, nearby banks whitened, turning into snow cliffs. Running swiftly downward, the energy froze the river itself into an icy channel.

The amount of energy required to work this deadly miracle was phenomenal, but Freeze's power gems were well able to provide it.

Within minutes, the entire observatory was transformed into a fortress of ice.

"I'm glad you came," Ivy whispered. She and Robin sat together on the platform, Ivy leaning seductively close to the young hero. "I can't breathe without you."

Robin regarded her seriously. "I want us to be together, but I need to know you mean it about turning over a new leaf. I need a sign."

Mischief twinkled in Ivy's eyes. "How about 'Dangerous Curves'?" she teased.

"A sign of trust," Robin persisted. "Tell me your plan."

"Kiss me and I'll tell you," Ivy said coquettishly.

"Tell me and I'll kiss you," Robin shot back.

Ivy shrugged. What difference would it make if Robin knew? Soon he would be like putty in her hands.

"Freeze has transformed the new telescope into a Freezing Gun," she explained. "He's about to turn Gotham City into an ice cube."

Robin recoiled. "I've got to stop him!"

Ivy grasped his arm, pulling him down toward her. "One kiss, my love. For luck."

It seemed as if Robin couldn't resist. Their faces came together, and his eyes closed as their lips met.

Ivy pulled back first, a smug look on her face. "Bad

luck, I'm afraid," she said contentedly. "It's time to die, little bird. You should have heeded your pointy-eared pal." She touched a finger to her lips. "These lips can be murder."

"Then . . . you never loved me?" Robin choked the words out.

Ivy looked at him disdainfully. "Love you?" she scoffed, allowing her true feelings to surface for the first time. "I loathe your bipedal arrogance, your animal superiority. My only joy is knowing that even now, my poison kiss is sucking the life from your apelike face!"

Her eyes widened with surprise as a voice behind her said, "I'm not saying I told you so."

Batman walked from the shadows where he'd concealed himself after following Robin to Blossom Street. It was easy for one with his skills to enter undetected.

"You're too late," Ivy hissed. "Say bye-bye, birdie!"

But Robin didn't look as if he'd been poisoned. In fact, he was grinning. "Sorry to disappoint you, Ivy," he said triumphantly. He reached up, grasped his lip, pulled — and a strip of thin latex coating came away in his hand. "Rubber lips are immune to your charms!"

Ivy stared, dumbstruck, as Batman explained: "Robin and I found the cure to your evil spell. And that's teamwork."

Suddenly the villainess screamed, her rage pouring from her in one awful, high-pitched shriek. She shoved Robin hard, and he fell back into the lily pool with a splash. Immediately, predatory vines snaked to entangle him.

More vines sent tendrils and branches shooting out to wrap around Batman. He snapped a few, but more grew to take their place, and within seconds he was engulfed in vicious vegetation. He felt himself wrenched off his feet, hanging upside down as the shoots and stalks did their best to squeeze the life from him.

"Sorry, boys," Ivy said with total insincerity. "My vines seem to have a crush on you!"

She leaped onto a massive lily pad, skipping off onto another before the first could sink. "Gotta run. So many people to kill. So little time."

Above her, the skylight shattered without warning. Bright moonlight streamed in, illuminating the dark-clad figure that descended from above. It wore a long cape and a sleek eye-mask, and landed gracefully in front of Poison Ivy.

Batgirl was on her very first mission.

"You're about to become compost," she threatened. She defended herself expertly as Ivy launched a furious martial arts assault. Kicking, chopping, striking, blocking, the two young women fought in a blur.

Above them, Batman had managed to draw a slim knife

from his Utility Belt and was desperately hacking at the clinging vines. In the lily pond, Robin struggled to free himself from the aquatic stems that imprisoned him.

"Using feminine wiles to get what you want," Batgirl said, blocking a side kick. "Trading on your looks. Exploiting men's weakness. Read a book, sister." She grunted with satisfaction as her own blow struck home on Ivy's arm. "That nonsense went out in the seventies. Chicks like you give women a bad name!"

Batgirl retreated as Ivy redoubled her attack, backing the new heroine against the wall.

Ivy smiled in anticipation of victory. "As I told Lady Freeze when I pulled her plug," she said smugly, "this is a one-woman show!"

"I don't think so." Batgirl avoided the blow, and grabbed Ivy by the hair. Jerking down hard, she brought up her knee to connect with Ivy's forehead. The plant woman swayed, then slumped to the floor, unconscious.

Batgirl was already cuffing her when Batman finally dropped to the floor and Robin crawled from the pool.

"And you are?" Batman asked.

"Batgirl." She lifted the mask for a moment. "It's me. Barbara. I found the Batcave!"

"We gotta get those locks changed!" Robin joked.

Minutes later, the three heroes raced into the Gotham night.

CHAPTER

15

Lights flashing, sirens wailing, a squad of police cruisers screamed up the sloping avenue toward the observatory.

"One-Adam-twelve, one-Adam-twelve, see the mad scientist with the freezing ray!" Perched high on the platform, Freeze and Bane watched the cavalcade draw quickly closer. Freeze leaned over to touch the metal barrel of the telescope. "Cops on the rocks, anyone?"

A huge blue beam of cryonic energy streaked toward the street below. Instantly, the police cars turned into screeching, skidding cubes of solid ice. Out of control, their occupants flash-frozen, they crashed and slammed into each other. Two cars exploded in a raging fireball.

"Police are so hot-tempered these days." Freeze turned to his brawny companion. "Don't you agree, Mr. Bane?"

The masked monster gave no indication it had even heard.

The banks of the Gotham River were like a scene from the frozen wastes of the Arctic. Thick snow covered everything. Icicles five feet long hung from the trees, and a thick sheet of ice had formed over the water itself.

Down this frozen highway the Batsled moved with speed, Robin at its helm. The sleek, one-man ice sail seemed to dance over the frozen river as Robin expertly kept it on an even keel.

There was a muffled roar, and the Bathammer raced to join the sled. An all-white Batmobile had been mounted on rocket skis, and though it lacked the grace of the Batsled, it more than compensated with sheer power.

A third craft moved to join them. Batgirl straddled the single-bladed rocket snowcycle known as the Batblade, taking up position on the flank.

The little armada raced along the surface of the frozen water, toward the ice-swept observatory.

They didn't come unnoticed. Freeze had his eye to the telescope's viewfinder. His expression darkened as he saw the three vehicles speeding his way.

"So Ivy failed to unmask Batman and Robin," he stated. "No matter. The Bat and the Bird are mine at last." He operated the mechanism that tilted the telescope, its huge barrel seesawing on its central pivot. Now it pointed directly down into the heart of Gotham City. "Watch, Batman, as your beloved Gotham freezes. And prepare to die. Because you're next!"

Blue cryonic rays leaped downward on their mission of death.

On the city streets, people went about their lives unaware. They were walking dogs, drinking on stoops, eating in diners, lounging on corners, kissing against alley walls. The blue glow washed over them all, freezing them, turning the streets and buildings into glistening ice.

"The Bat-talion approaches," Freeze said, cracking another bad pun, then snapped into his radio, "Icemen — attack!"

Freeze's minions had been awaiting his signal. A specially adapted truck burst from its hiding place on the riverbank, blasting toward the Bat-team on high blades. Two pairs of Icemen hung from towlines, their skis hissing as they maneuvered behind the truck. Their machine guns blazed into life.

In the cockpit of the Bathammer, monitor screens mapped the truck's approach. "Attack plan Alpha," Batman barked into his communicator.

Immediately the Batsled peeled off to the side. "Alpha. Roger," Robin's voice came over the intercom.

On the back of the speeding Batblade, Batgirl nodded. "Alpha. Got it." Her eyebrows wrinkled under her mask and cowl. "Um . . . what exactly is attack plan Alpha?"

"Divide and conquer," Robin's voice informed her. Batgirl veered her craft off to the opposite side in sudden realization.

A pair of skiing Icemen whipped toward her, their guns spitting shells that chewed up the ice around her craft.

A second pair of skiers had targeted Robin, heading directly for his billowing sail, a blizzard of shots searing the air around him.

And as for the Bathammer, Freeze had a very special welcome for it. He punched a button, and remote-controlled side-mounted rocket launchers spat their deadly cargo from the truck. Batman swerved as the rockets exploded in front of him, punching hissing holes in the thick ice. He careened around them, gunning the Bathammer's turbos, heading straight for the modified truck.

Off to the side, the two Icemen bearing down on Robin suddenly released their tethers. Their guns chattered wildly as they converged on the sled. Robin heaved on the boom and the Batsled's sail luffed. The vehicle changed direction abruptly, the two skiers missing it by inches. They didn't even have time to be surprised before they slammed into each other with bone-jarring force.

Dodging bullets, Batgirl scanned the status panel

menu of the Batblade's special modifications. "Nice extras package," she noted, selecting the setting marked ICE CUTTER.

At once the Batblade's scythelike keel peeled back, revealing an even sharper blade beneath. Spinning and side-kicking, Batgirl used her deft driving skills to send a wave of frozen ice into the faces of her attackers. Unable to avoid it, they tumbled in backward somersaults across the ice.

"That's what I call a close shave!" She said with a giggle.

The ice truck's guns blazed as the Bathammer inexorably homed in on it. Batman held his course steady, right hand reaching out, finger stabbing a control button.

Twin torpedoes shot out from under the Bathammer's chassis, snaking across the ice to detonate directly in front of the truck. Ice flew in all directions as a tremendous explosion erupted. The driver wasn't able to swerve in time. The truck hit the steaming pool and flipped up nose first, starting to sink into the icy waters.

Icemen scrabbled to safety as the Bathammer shot past.

Mr. Freeze had watched the battle from the platform high above. Now he tilted the giant telescope further, directly toward the river below. "Not so fast," he said quietly, though the trio in the vehicles below couldn't hear him. "It's time you cooled your heels."

The huge freeze-gun pulsed again. Its beam struck the frozen channel ahead of the Bat-force, and a high wall of rock-hard ice formed, completely blocking the river.

But the Bathammer had been modified to meet every possible situation. Batman operated another control, this one marked EMERGENCY BURN. The engines roared as the overdrive engaged, propelling the craft forward even faster. It raced at the ice wall like a missile, and burst through it in an explosion of ice.

The Batblade and Batsled shot up the face of the wall on either side of the gap, soaring high over the top of the mountain of ice.

They hit the frozen river on the other side together, whipping back into formation beside the Bathammer, for all the world as if they'd never split up.

Freeze stared at a monitor screen. The Bat-team had reached the base of the giant ice cliffs beneath the observatory. They were proving to have more endurance than he'd given them credit for.

"I'll finish off the city, Bane," the villain snapped. "You, as they say in show biz, are on. Kill the kids. But bring me the Bat."

The masked monster moved off. Ivy had ordered him to obey Freeze until her return. He would do so . . . or die.

At the base of the cliff, Batman slid out of the Bathammer. He glanced at the digital display on his watch. 11:49. "We have exactly eleven minutes to stop Freeze and thaw the city!"

Batgirl's and Robin's faces fell. Eleven minutes? Surely it was an impossible task!

CHAPTER

16

Using pitons and ropes, the Bat-team set out to scale the ice cliff as quickly as they could.

"This is easy," Batgirl said, laughing, as she hauled herself up hand over hand.

Robin shook his head ruefully. "Crimefighters' rule number one: Never say that."

"Why?" Batgirl asked.

Whooping and yelling, a score of Freeze's thugs poured over the edge of a ledge above. Their ropes secured safely above them, they slid down toward the heroes with guns ablaze.

"That's why," Robin said grimly. He swung wide on his rope as an Iceman plunged toward them, gun chattering, bullets biting chunks out of the cliff.

Robin grabbed Batgirl and hauled her with him — just in time. A line of hot lead chewed up the ice where she'd stood. They hit a snowbank and rolled together.

"Does this mean we're going steady?" Batgirl couldn't help asking as they tumbled to a stop. But the lightness in her voice died away as another four Icemen landed on the snow close to them.

Trusting the duo to take care of themselves, his every thought focused on saving Gotham City, Batman struggled upward. He pulled himself onto a ledge just below the observatory, reaching for a Batarang as several more Icemen descended out of the mist.

Batman paused, then resheathed the weapon. "Let's do this the old-fashioned way."

He strode into them like a whirlwind, fists and feet driving like pistons in an extended martial arts routine. It looked simple, but had taken years to perfect. Icemen dropped like ninepins, felled by the ferocity of his blows.

Fifty feet below, Robin and Batgirl were fighting back to back, heavily outnumbered by the squad of Icemen who surrounded them. Robin glanced up, and noticed a heavily cantilevered overhang of snow.

"Crimefighters' rule number two," he said to Barbara. "I'm afraid to ask!"

"Be ready for anything." Robin cupped his hands together and yelled through them as loud as he could. The effect was startling. The echo raced up the hill, to be answered a split second later by a dangerous rumbling. The Icemen looked up, but it was too late. An avalanche of snow and ice thundered into them as the overhang collapsed, sweeping them helplessly away down the slope.

Robin and Batgirl dealt summarily with the few survivors, then set out again for the summit.

Batman pulled himself up onto the aperture ledge as Robin and Batgirl climbed in from the other side. The giant telescope was still aimed down at Gotham — but the chamber was empty.

"No sign of the snowman." Batman cast his eyes around the room.

"Maybe he's melted," Robin replied.

Batman fired a grapple into the ceiling and swung across the room. He dropped two thermal mini-charges at the feet of the frozen scientists, and continued to swing on to the telescope platform itself. As Batgirl and Robin joined him, the Bat-charges began to glow.

It was close for the scientists; they were within seconds of passing the eleven-minute deadline that would have meant remaining frozen for all eternity. But the heat radiating from the Bat-charges swiftly melted and revived them.

"I hope you've got about ten million more of those little toys," Robin remarked dryly. He glanced at the control console clock. 11:52. "Only eight more minutes, and a cityful of Gothamites are ice cubes forever."

Batman looked thoughtful. "Sunlight could reverse the freezing process," he began.

"Sunrise isn't for five hours," Batgirl pointed out.

"Here," Batman replied.

Robin caught on immediately. "But it's already morning in the Congo!"

Batman nodded, pointing to a screen graphic showing the satellites in orbit. "If we could relay the sunlight," he went on, "from the other side of the equator . . ."

Batgirl grasped what he was getting at. "It'll take the satellites about a minute to realign —" She broke off, gazing out at the two small mirrors that were housed on the telescope barrel. Both were encased in ice. "But the targeting mirrors are frozen. The thawing beam won't work."

"I'll set the telescope," Batman said decisively. "You two thaw the mirrors."

Batgirl and Robin clambered up onto the telescope barrel, and hurried along it. As one, they removed miniature lasers from their Utility Belts. "I love this belt," Batgirl enthused. "Can I have a matching handbag?"

The lasers flared into life as the duo bent to their task.

At the main control console, Batman's hands flew over the keyboard.

Twenty-two thousand miles above the Earth, on the very edge of space, the chain of satellites received a coded radio signal. Their thrusters fired, bright against the inky darkness beyond, and the orbital mirrors began to turn.

The motion was reflected on the console screen. But Batman had no time for self-congratulation. The clock read 11:54. Time was running out. Fast.

Batman sighted up through a long cylinder, aiming the telescope. But the skyline he saw through the crosshairs blurred suddenly, as Mr. Freeze dropped onto the telescope from his hiding place in the rafters. His face loomed huge in the targeting scope.

"Tonight's forecast," he snarled. "A freeze is coming!"

The villain lunged and grabbed Batman, the extra strength provided by his suit allowing him to flip the hero up over his head onto the telescope barrel. Using his free hand, Freeze yanked on the telescope control joystick.

The huge barrel tilted sharply downward, snow and ice flying off it like a miniature blizzard.

Halfway up the barrel, Batgirl and Robin were caught unawares. Thrown off balance, they tumbled down the barrel, rolling toward the lens. It pointed out of the dome aperture, straight down at the city.

Fifteen feet above them, Batman managed to right his own fall. He tried to get a grip on the slippery surface. He hesitated for a millisecond as his mind weighed the situation. Below him, unable to stop themselves, Robin and Batgirl were sliding toward the end of the barrel. But above him, Freeze was climbing to the control console.

No way he could get to both. And there wasn't much time left.

Batman turned, and rushed up the barrel after Freeze.

He didn't look back as Robin and Batgirl shot off the end of the barrel, and started to drop. It had taken a lot, but Batman had trust in his partner — and Robin didn't let him down. Robin's grapple shot upward, to snag on a glacier-like overhang. The line jerked taut, just as Robin reached to grip Batgirl's wrist.

They hung there for a moment, suspended. "I've got you," Robin assured her.

Suddenly, his grapple broke free of the ice that anchored it, and they began to plunge again. But this time it was Batgirl who fired a Batarang with line attached. It found a solid hold in an icy cleft, and the duo jerked to a halt again as the line held.

"No. *I've* got *you*." Batgirl smiled.

Frantically, Mr. Freeze operated the main telescope controls. On the monitor screen, the satellite schematics flashed red. A message showed: TARGET LOCK DISABLED.

The clock read 11:56. Four more minutes before Gotham was doomed forever.

From the corner of his eye, Freeze saw Batman rush up the telescope toward him. The villain hit another control, and at once the giant telescope began to swing and tilt madly about its pivot. Batman fought desperately for balance, arms flailing. He'd come so close . . . he couldn't fail now!

A mighty leap carried him off the bucking barrel and onto the control platform. "Millions will die," he said, advancing grimly on Freeze. "Isn't that taking all this a little too far?"

The villain drew his pistol in one quick motion, aiming it at Batman. "We aim to freeze," he said, grinning.

A bolt of solid cold lanced at Batman, who deflected it at the last moment with his suit armor. But the impact knocked him off his feet. He fell heavily, grabbing at the telescope frame. Freeze fired again, and Batman had to let go and drop to avoid the fierce ice blast.

His hands closed on a service plate, and he hung there beneath the telescope, upside down.

Freeze lost no time. "Let's swing," he invited, whirling the control joystick around. He laughed as the telescope followed suit, twisting and bucking like a rodeo bronco. Batman clung on for dear life.

The two scientists on the tower platform had recovered by now. They gasped as they saw the telescope barrel swinging wildly toward them, Batman hanging on.

"It's just one of those days," one scientist groaned.

The telescope smashed directly into the platform with a terrible crash, and the whole structure began to topple. The scientists leaped up as the platform thudded heavily to the floor below. They landed safely on the swinging telescope, clinging grimly on to the tensioning bar.

Freeze cursed as the juddering impact threw him off his feet and into the telescope platform rail. His gun dropped from his grip, and landed at his feet.

Shaken loose, Batman was plummeting toward the observatory floor. A Batarang flashed from his hand, and his fall stopped short just in time as his line swung him up and away. Three more feet and he'd have smashed into the floor.

As Freeze bent to pick up his gun, Batman swung into him with full force. His feet hit the villain squarely, sending him flying to the back of the telescope.

Seizing his opportunity, Batman began to type commands into the console. The telescope slowed, and stopped its crazy spinning. On the screen, the satellite graphics flashed green. The clock read 11:58.

The mirrors overhead started to glow, flooding with sunlight. The mere sight of the light sent Freeze into a frenzy. Screaming with rage, he stunned Batman with a two-handed blow. He grabbed the hero and raised him over his head. Without even pausing to utter one of his trademark one-liners, Freeze hurled the Dark Knight down the telescope barrel.

As he plunged wildly toward the base of the aperture slit, Batman could see the lights of Gotham far below him.

CHAPTER

17

Bracing himself as best he could for the impact, Batman slammed painfully onto the end of the telescope barrel. Carefully getting to his feet, he balanced there, sizing up the situation.

"Wow. Batman!" The two scientists were clinging to a targeting groove on the body of the barrel, not sure whether to be terrified because of the danger or excited by the most adventurous situation they'd ever been in. And now Batman was here, too.

Way above, Batman could see that Freeze was back at the control console. "Can you give me any more height on this thing?" he asked. One of the scientists nodded enthusiastically.

He stretched down to pull on a red emergency override lever, and suddenly the telescope reversed itself. It tilted straight up, at full speed, sending Batman soaring into the air toward the dome above.

The crimefighter somersaulted in midair, and landed

precisely where he wanted: directly behind Freeze on the control platform. The blade of his hand swept down, striking the villain hard on the upper arm.

Freeze swung to face him, unleashing a blow that would have taken Batman's head clean off . . . if Batman had waited for it to land. But he ducked beneath it, his fists striking hard into his enemy's stomach.

"You've turned Gotham to ice," Batman accused, aiming a crescent kick high on Freeze's leg. "You've endangered countless lives." A straight-arm blow to the villain's helmet. "It's payback time."

They swung and kicked and punched like men possessed. Batman represented the apex of human development, the perfect athlete in perfect condition. But Freeze had trained long and hard for years, and even though his cryo-suit had been damaged in the fight, he had the benefit of its power.

They fought like warriors — like titans — one bent on destroying Gotham, the other on saving it.

Using the rail for support, Freeze struck out with a double-footed kick that took Batman squarely in the chest. He toppled back off the platform. He'd performed the stunt so many times, it had become automatic: a Batarang flashed from his hand, trailing its tough metal-fiber line. The line whipped around the platform rail, then arced on to loop itself around Freeze's neck.

The villain lurched off the platform, his plunging body acting like a counterweight. Batman soared up. Freeze landed painfully on his engine of cold as Batman landed again on the platform.

Overhead, the mirrors finally aligned. Beams of concentrated sunlight angled down, striking the Freezing Engine . . . and its maker. Freeze quivered as bright sunlight bathed him, penetrating the rips and tears in his damaged suit.

Then the telescope activated, and a powerful thawing beam shot from its huge lens. Steam hissed up from where it struck, and Batman heaved a sigh of relief. At last, it was over.

He looked down at Freeze, who was coughing and spluttering in the sunlight, his white skin starting to gray and wither.

"You're losing your cool," Batman couldn't resist saying.

Shrugging off the debilitating pain of the heat, Freeze disagreed. "I think not. There'll be no hot time in the old town tonight." He pulled out a remote control device, and thumbed the button that primed it. "You'll get a real charge out of this!"

The explosives, which Bane had set earlier, now blew in a series of fiery blooms. Taking advantage of Batman's confusion, Freeze rolled to the side, out of the murderous sunlight. He dropped to the floor below as the remaining charges went off around the telescope's base.

The huge structure tilted, hung for a second in the air, then dropped out of the open viewing aperture toward the city below.

Robin and Batgirl had pulled themselves onto an ice ledge and were making their way up to the dome slat when the telescope plunged past them. Batman and the two scientists clung grimly to it.

Robin's mouth opened to cry "Batman!" — but he broke off at Batgirl's startled call.

"Please tell me he's on our side," the girl gasped. A huge figure moved out from behind an ice rock, fists closing and unclosing, muscles rippling, face hidden behind his gruesome mask — Bane.

The crimefighter coiled into a spinning roundhouse kick. Bane blocked it easily, and knocked him away. Robin fell back hard into the ice as Bane advanced on Batgirl.

The telescope plunged down through the air, gathering speed. Batman slid down to join the scientists. As he dropped, he fired a double-ended tether, a grapple shooting out horizontally to either side. They sank deep into the arms of the gargantuan sculpture that held up the entire observatory, just as the telescope plummeted past.

"Grab my belt and hang on," Batman rasped. The scientists hurried to do his bidding, fighting for balance as the rushing air tried to claw them off.

Robin shook off the effects of Bane's blow, struggling to his feet. Batgirl was fending off Bane with a series of fast kicks and punches. But she might as well have been hitting steel, for all the effect she was having.

She glanced at the recovering Robin, and called: "Don't worry. I've got him!"

Just then Bane grabbed her by the throat and slammed her into an ice wall. He pulled back his huge fist, ready to deliver the killing blow.

"No — *I've* got him," Robin yelled. He leaped up onto the monster's back, grabbing at the tubes that led from Bane's injector pack into his skull. Milky-white Venom sprayed wildly in the air as Robin yanked them off.

Bane went down in a heap, throwing the boy clear. The criminal's body writhed and spasmed as the effect of the Venom was reversed. His muscles convulsed and shrank before the amazed eyes of Robin and Batgirl. He groaned and screamed with pain, until finally he was just Antonio Diego again, a scrawny prisoner struggling in the folds of a costume many sizes too large.

The scientists held tight to Batman's belt as the cable pulled taut. The telescope dropped away from under them as the line bent like a bow, Batman and the scientists sinking at its center.

The cable reached its nadir over an outcrop of rock on the icy cliff. Far below, the telescope splintered into a million pieces as it slammed into the frozen river with breathtaking force.

"This is your stop." Batman shoved the scientists off onto the ledge. Freed of their weight, the line tautened at once. Batman was sent rocketing up through the air like an arrow from a bow.

He flipped in through the telescope slat just as Batgirl and Robin finally arrived. The trio landed together on the observatory floor.

"Only seconds to midnight," Batgirl gasped in horror. "The telescope's gone. There's no way to thaw the city!"

Batman disagreed. "Theoretically, the satellites could be positioned to thaw the city directly. But it would take a computer genius."

Robin was already heading for the console. "I'm on it!" He cleared debris from the surface, and started to type into the keyboard. Nothing. The equipment was dead.

"No, *I'm* on it." Batgirl shouldered him roughly aside, knowing there wasn't a second to spare. Quickly, she patched together some broken wires. The console lit up, whirring into life again. Batgirl's hands flew over the board, hitting key after key, as she hacked into the operating system.

Up beyond the stratosphere, the giant orbital satellites finally aligned. A full disc of sun appeared in one of the precision-polished mirrors. It was beamed instantly on to the next in the relay, then the next. Within seconds, the concentrated beam was slicing down toward Gotham City.

Wherever the wide rays of focused sunshine struck, the ice melted in pools of hissing steam. People suddenly found themselves dripping wet, coming back from the brink of the icy fate that had awaited them. Whole streets sprang back to life as the warming rays passed over them.

Mr. Freeze lay in the rubble, weak and gray, struggling to breathe in the growing heat. "Go on — kill me, too," he snarled. "Just as you killed my wife."

"I didn't kill your wife." Batman pressed a button on his Utility Belt, and rapped: "Run Ivy evidence tape 001.4."

A tiny monitor set in Batman's gauntlet blinked on. He held it down so Freeze could see the miniature image of Poison Ivy within.

"As I told Lady Freeze when I pulled the plug," her recorded voice was saying, "this is a one-woman show."

Freeze opened his mouth and screamed. His face streamed with frozen tears, glittering on his cheek like diamonds.

"She's not dead, Victor," Batman calmed him. "We found her and restored her icy slumber. She's still frozen, but alive, waiting for you to find a cure."

Freeze could hardly believe it. "She lives," he said weakly. "She lives!"

"Vengeance isn't power," Batman went on. "Anyone with a gun can take a life. To give life — that's true power. So I'm asking you now, Victor Fries, to save another's life." Batman's eyes met Freeze's, and held his gaze. "Show me how to cure McGregor's Syndrome Stage One. And perhaps you can also save the man your wife once loved. He's still inside you, buried deep beneath the ice. Will you help me?" Batman's voice dropped. "Doctor?"

Freeze stared at his captor, his sworn enemy, for a long moment. Then he unsealed his chestplate and removed two glowing power orbs. He held them out to Batman, his smile bittersweet.

"Take two of these," he said weakly, "and call me in the morning."

CHAPTER

18

It was four in the morning. The time they say the human spirit is at its lowest ebb.

Three figures stood around Alfred's bed, not speaking, their breathing hushed so as not to disturb the old butler's shallow, fitful sleep. Silently, Batman brought out the modified gems that Freeze had given him. Batgirl and Robin watched as he carefully attached them to a slot in Alfred's life support system.

"All we can do now is wait," Batman whispered. He reached down to take Alfred's hand. "And hope."

The guards had been doubled at Arkham Asylum. No one would be escaping again from there in a hurry.

Poison Ivy sat in her cramped cell, in barred moonlight,

staring out the window. She held a small flower in her hand. Absentmindedly, she pulled the petals off, one by one.

"He loves me, he loves me not," she intoned with each petal. "He loves me, he loves me —"

"Not," a cold voice finished for her.

Ivy turned in surprise. Mr. Freeze stood there, in full costume. He indicated it with a sweep of his hand. "It's amazing what you can buy around here for a few dozen diamonds."

He took a step toward her, and Ivy flinched. There was nothing organic in the cell, nothing she could warp and mutate and coerce into working for her. Freeze took another step, a terrible smile on his face.

"Prepare for a bitter harvest," he told her. "Winter has come at last."

Dawn rose over Wayne Manor, the sun's rosy rays heralding a new day.

A bright new day, Bruce Wayne hoped, as sunlight dancing through the half-closed drapes lit up the room. It looked like World War III had been fought — and lost — there. Pizza cartons and soda cans were strewn everywhere. Barbara sprawled on a couch, dozing lightly. Dick

Grayson paced up and down, anxiety etched on every feature.

Bruce walked to the window and stared out over the grounds. He would give up all of this — the house, the landscaped gardens, the priceless antiques — if only it would keep Alfred alive. For in truth, none of it would mean anything without him.

Bruce frowned. He thought he'd heard a small cough. Like Alfred's. Bruce shook his head, to clear his fuddled senses.

The cough came again, louder now.

"Ahem."

Barbara leaped awake, and all three turned to look through the open doorway to the stairs. Alfred was descending, a scowl like thunder on his brow.

"Alfred!" Bruce greeted him. "Are you . . . ?"

"Rather disappointed at how poorly I taught you housekeeping." Alfred sniffed. "But otherwise — I'm quite well again." He paused, then added in a gentler voice, "Thanks to you, son." He smiled radiantly at Bruce, and looked to Dick and Barbara. "Thanks to all of you."

All three moved toward him, to hug him, to welcome him back into the family.

Dick turned to Bruce. "One question. When Batgirl and I rolled off the telescope, how come you didn't try and save us? It was the first time I fell and you weren't there to catch me."

"I knew you could handle it," Bruce said simply. Then, quoting Robin's words of a few days ago: "Sometimes counting on someone else is the only way to win."

Barbara swelled with pride. "Hey, I'm the one who kicked Ivy's botanical rear end," she boasted. "Me. Personally. I did."

Bruce regarded her thoughtfully. "You, young lady, are going back to school."

"I wouldn't count on that," Dick broke in, remembering what Barbara had told him. "Wouldn't surprise me if she's going to be sticking around."

Barbara extended her hand. "Partners?" she asked.

For an awful moment, she thought the others were going to say no. Her heart leaped into her mouth. She'd been here such a short time, and yet . . . it felt like coming home.

But then, first Dick's hand, then Bruce's came out to clasp hers.

"Partners," both men said together.

Alfred rolled his eyes in mock despair. "There's only one thing," he sighed. "We're going to need a bigger cave!"

Darkness had barely fallen the next night when the Bat-Signal shone from the roof of police headquarters. The Commissioner needed help. The city was in danger.

But this time, the two heroes who raced to answer the call had another by their side. The villains of Gotham City would soon learn to fear the name of Batgirl, as they already feared Batman and Robin.

A new team was born.

ABOUT THE AUTHOR

ALAN GRANT was born in Bristol, England, in 1949. His grandmother taught him to read at the age of three, using *Batman* and other adventure comics as her textbooks, and he has been a comics fanatic ever since. He left school when he was seventeen to pursue a career in accounting, but quickly realized he'd made a mistake and switched to publishing. After editing wildlife, romance, and fashion magazines, he quit to go freelance and produced a successful run of teenage true confession stories before returning to his first love: comics. With longtime writing partner John Wagner, he scripted *Judge Dredd* and a dozen other science fiction series for the British comic book sensation *2000 AD*. This work brought him to the attention of *Batman* editor Dennis O'Neil, and in the nine years since then, Alan has written more than a hundred *Batman* stories. He is currently the regular writer of *Batman: Shadow of the Bat* (sixty-five issues and counting!) and *Lobo* for DC Comics, and is working on a top-secret project with John Wagner and fan-favorite artist Simon Bisley. His previous two Batman novels — *Batman: Knightfall & Beyond* and *Batman Forever* — were both bestsellers. Mr. Grant lives and works in a Gothic mansion in the Scottish border country, with his wife and guardian angel, Sue.

Collect all the latest action-packed
BATMAN & ROBIN
books!

BATMAN & ROBIN

BATGIRL:
TO DARE THE DARKNESS

ROBIN:
FACING THE ENEMY

And don't miss the adaptation of the animated
direct-to-video motion picture
SubZero